H·M·C

HEALTH MANAGEMENT CORPORATION

PRESENTS

THE FATHERHOOD FAZE

BY

CONNIE MARSHALL R.N., M.S.N.

CONMAR PUBLISHING, INC.
P.O. BOX 641
CITRUS HEIGHTS, CA 95611
(916) 332-9872

Benefits That Deliver Before You Do

Composition by Conmar Publishing, Inc.
Production by Carol Dondrea, Bookman Productions
Copyediting by Eva Marie Strock
Interior Design by Renee Deprey
Cover design by The Dunlavey Studio
Cover Illustration by Terry Hoff

Prima Publishing
Rocklin, CA

In agreement with:
Conmar Publishing, Inc.
P.O. Box 641
Citrus Heights, CA 95611
1-800-428-8321

Library of Congress Cataloging-in-Publication Data

Marshall, Connie C. (Connie Clydene).
   The expectant father/Connie Marshall
      p.   cm.
   Includes index.
   ISBN 1-55958-219-7 (pbk.)
   1. Pregnancy. 2. Childbirth. 3. Fathers.   I. Title.
RG525.M3328   1992
618.2′4—dc20   92-18026
                                                          CIP

92 93 94 **RRD** 10 9 8 7 6 5 4 3 2

Printed in the United States of America

TABLE OF CONTENTS

PART I
REORGANIZATON

PART II
PLANNING AND DEVELOPMENT

PART III
IMPLEMENTATION

DEDICATION

This book is dedicated to the memory of Bob Anderson, a loving husband, father, and associate whose untimely passing is felt by all of us who had the pleasure of knowing him. We will miss you, Bob, but your kindness of spirit will live on forever.

Kathi and Connie Marshall

ΔΔΔ

ACKNOWLEDGMENTS

To Cheryl, who can do anything and never says "no." She cheerfully added research assistant to her ever expanding job description, and recruited expectant fathers from her prepared childbirth classes to share their perceptions and experiences with us.

To Kathi, for her unique gift of connecting with talented people and convincing them to share their expertise with us.

To Dr. Ronald Levant, and James Levine, pioneers in the fatherhood movement, who reviewed the manuscript and gave valuable input and support.

A special thanks to the staff of Health Management Corporation and the health education department of Empire Blue Cross and Blue Shield for their valuable input throughout each stage of this book.

The most special thanks and very grateful appreciation goes to all the expectant fathers who shared their feelings, fears, fun times, and photographs with us during their journey to fatherhood, so that same path for other expectant fathers might be less bumpy.

ΔΔΔ

PREFACE

If you are interested in this book, you are probably standing on the threshold of fatherhood. Perhaps your wife is expecting, or maybe the two of you are still in the "planning" stages. This might not be your first child, but if not, it's probably a good bet that you are approaching this situation with a good deal more deliberation and involvement than before.

As you contemplate your future role as someone's dad, you may wonder what kind of father you are going to be. For the current generation of fathers, this is an especially difficult task because we are expected to enact very different roles than the ones for which we were prepared by our parents. Nowadays, fathers are given the choice between the morning shift—getting the breakfasts and lunches made, getting the kids dressed and off to day care or school, or the evening shift—getting dinner started and the kids settled in their homework and evening routines.

However, most of us were raised to be just like our dads, whose job it was to keep a roof over our heads and put bread on the table. Dad only got involved when we did something we shouldn't (Remember being told "wait 'till your father gets home?") Our parents expected that as adults we would live more or less like they did. They had no idea that the Ozzie and Harriet model of breadwinner-husband and homemaker-mother would, in the space of a generation, become nearly extinct as a family form. They could not anticipate the women's movement and the divorce revolution, and their enormous impact on our social landscape.

Not only were we encouraged to model ourselves after our fathers, we were also put on a gender-based socialization track, which avoided certain experiences that might have better prepared us for an involved father role. We did not play with dolls, nor mind our younger siblings when our parents were unavailable, nor go to home economics classes, nor offer babysitting services to our neighbors. When our sisters' girl scout troops visited nursing homes and practiced the skill of nurturing, we huddled in the woods learning to start a cooking fire by rubbing sticks together.

Thus, becoming a father, in today's terms, is not an easy task for the current generation of fathers. We simply did not have the experiential foundation that would have allowed an easier transition into the role. Resources are clearly needed. *The Expectant Father* is, for many fathers, just what the doctor ordered: A comprehensive book on pregnancy, childbirth, and the postpartum period, *written just for men*. The topics discussed, the organization of the book, and the style of presentation all reflect the author's intention of creating a book that addresses the entire experience of becoming a family from the male perspective. While much of the information contained within is equally important for mothers, it is nonetheless presented in a way that speaks to the concerns that men are likely to have. I certainly wish that such a resource were available when my daughter was born.

Dr. Ronald F. Levant, Ed.D.
faculty, Cambridge Hospital/Harvard University
Co-author of Between Father and Child
Past director of the Fatherhood Project at Boston University
Editor for the *Journal of Family Psychology*

INTRODUCTION

The positive pregnancy test officially sets you on the path to fatherhood. Your life is changed forever. You may have great hopes for the kind of father you want to be, but the road ahead of you can seem hazy. How do you get there from here? You need all the help you can get.

You may not be physically pregnant, but you are psychologically and emotionally going through your own unique changes and adjustments as you move into this new phase in your life.

The prospect of fatherhood, with all its ramifications and responsibilities, can faze, deter, daunt, and disconcert even the most stable of the male species. Pregnancy gives you the time to begin your inner search for your own unique fatherhood model. You probably have a lot of important reexamining and restructuring of your attitudes and belief systems to prepare that warm, nurturing, open, and intimate place for yourself in your child's heart and life.

A multitude of books on the market deal with pregnancy; most focus almost exclusively on the expectant mother's experience. You, the expectant father, are an afterthought if you're included at all. This book focuses on your particular needs, thoughts, and feelings as an expectant father. The goal is to help you recognize, understand, and cope more effectively with the profound changes you experience as you set upon the path of fatherhood. Every expectant father's experience is unique, but they all share some common ground during this time. To find that common ground, we solicited and invited expectant and new fathers to share their pregnancy experiences with us. They graciously shared the wide range of feelings, emotions, hopes, and fears they experienced from the moment they learned of their wife's pregnancy to those first few weeks after their baby arrived. We've used their thoughts and comments throughout the book to convey more vividly certain aspects of the pregnancy experience from the male viewpoint.

Expecting a baby can be a very intense experience for both you and your wife. Humor, now being recognized by the health care profession as a potent healer, is used throughout this book to help decrease your anxiety and balance your perspective between your needs and your wife's as you navigate the sometimes choppy waters of change. Humor is a helpful companion as you sail toward the harbor of parenthood together.

Even though you may not be married, in this book the mother of your child is referred to as "your wife" because the term has a nicer ring to it than "significant other," "lover", "partner," or "mate." The baby is alternately referred to as "he" and "she" to help keep your options open. Your wife's doctor is also alternately referred to as "he" and "she."

Since there is much more information needed regarding the expectant father and his experience during pregnancy and birth, we invite you to share your hopes, feelings, fears, and memorable pregnancy and early fatherhood experiences with us. We would like to add fresh perspectives and new comments with each new edition of this book. Address your correspondence to us at Conmar Publishing, Inc. P.O. Box 641, Citrus Heights, CA 95611.

Good luck. We wish the very best for you and your new family.

ΔΔΔ

PART 1

REORGANIZATION

1

ATTITUDES AND ADJUSTMENTS

PREGNANT PAUSE

When you get the good news the pregnancy test is positive, you can't help but pat yourself on the back for a job well done. Your pride swells as you feel a spiritual connection with all those creators of life before you. You feel immortal. Your friends and family share your joy at the news. One of them will probably smile and cryptically tell you that "Your life will never be the same again." You get the feeling that there's more behind that comment than meets the eye, but for now nothing can dampen your enthusiasm and excitement.

> **"I was so excited when we tested ourselves positive that I ran over and gave her a great big hug and told her how proud I was of her and me. I felt tears well up inside of me."**

The euphoria does subside in time, and you shift from feelings of immortality to the more mere mortal realities of the coming event and what it all means. Even if you had planned to start your family now, you slide into a minor state of shock.

You probably find yourself mentally previewing the potential changes that may occur in your life. The VCR of your mind fast forwards through the next 21 years of house payments, teen drivers, and college tuition in a dizzying collage of all that is possible.

> **"I worry about the financial concerns and having enough time to devote to family."**
>
> **"In the early months, I remember confusion and disbelief along with great joy. My initial reaction was surprise and shock."**

CHANGING TIMES

You naturally think about how a baby is going to change your relationship with your wife. You aren't sure what all those changes will entail or if you're quite ready for them. You aren't sure if they'll be wonderful or less than welcome.

> **"Even though I really wanted and even lobbied to have a baby, I wondered if we had done the right thing, afterall. I worried about my role as a father, if I would lose my freedom, how the baby would change my relationship with my wife, and would she ever look the same again."**
>
> **"It was a difficult adjustment to realize I was no longer king of the castle."**

Your inner child may be giving you messages that he isn't happy to be usurped even by your own child. Up to now you and your wife have enjoyed a certain amount of freedom, indulging yourselves as individuals and as a couple. You wonder how much you're going to have to give up. Dark thoughts about the health and safety of your wife and baby throughout pregnancy also seep into your thoughts. The uncertainty can leave you dizzy with dread. Don't be surprised if your brain freeze frames in self-defense. What have you gotten yourself into? You need space and time to sort out all this fatherhood stuff. Let the dust settle in your brain.

> **"I worried about my wife's health and the complexity of the fetal growth process."**
>
> **"In the beginning, I had lots of anxiety both good and bad. I was anxious to know about the baby, yet nervous about the responsibilities that lay ahead."**

The intensity of your feelings about your wife's pregnancy may be a little scary at first. Although our culture has come to accept a more nurturing role from men, you're not sure how that applies to you. Taking up a new hobby or going back to school are perfectly normal at this time. To keep your mind off the prospect of too much change all at once, you seek activities away from home and hearth for a while so you can sort through the future events. It doesn't mean that you aren't happy about the baby or you don't love your wife. The coming changes tug on your psyche, and you find yourself pulling back just a little for now. You're perfectly normal.

You're also normal if you totally embrace pregnancy and feel that you're both pregnant. You might even experience some nausea, put on a few pounds around your middle, and share some of your wife's physical complaints. This is called "couvade" a male pregnancy experience that different cultures have recognized for eons. You have a strong desire to share in the creation and growth of your child.

To add to the confusion, just about the time the news of your impending fatherhood sinks in, you notice that the mother of your unborn child seems to be weirding out in subtle and/or bizarre ways.

FRIENDLY FIRE

During pregnancy, your wife is working through internal changes referred to as developmental tasks. In the first trimester (3 months), she has to come to terms with and accept the reality of the pregnancy. Before she reaches that point, she deals with the same kind of ambivalence as you do, no matter how thrilled she is about being pregnant. Is this really the best thing for us? Maybe we should have waited a little longer? Can we really afford to have a baby? Am I really ready to be a mother?

First Trimester

In those first 3 months you can feel like you're in a battle zone. The hormones of pregnancy keep your wife emotionally and physically off balance. One minute she's Sally Sweetness, who cries over the beauty of the sunset, and in the next minute she seems more like the soul mate of Boris the pit bull chained next door. She worries about miscarrying and her thickening waistline. If that's not enough, she's also dealing with mind-numbing fatigue, sore breasts, and possibly nausea. She may not be feeling terribly social.

> **"I try to give her support for her ups and downs while improving my patience. I'll need it with the child too, so it's best to start now."**
>
> **"I ignore her ups and downs for the most part."**
>
> **"The worst part of pregnancy was her being sick so much. I felt so helpless."**

Be prepared to be caught in "friendly fire" from time to time. Be patient and don't worry. Remember, she isn't crazy, just pregnant. The condition is temporary.

Second Trimester

In the second trimester your wife worked through her ambivalence and now perceives the baby as part of her body; they are one. Emotionally she regains her internal balance. She can still have mood swings, but they aren't so dramatic. She craves your attention and reassurance that you still find her attractive and desirable.

> **"My most difficult adjustment has been getting used to my wife's 'new look'."**

Physically, she feels great. Her bustline blossoms, but so does her waist. Most women come to terms with the physical changes pregnancy brings to their bodies; others don't fare as well and grieve actively for their lost figure and the altered body image that pregnancy brings. It can be a very sensitive subject with many pregnant women. This is not the time to make jokes about her expanding middle or express your concerns about her regaining her figure after pregnancy, however harmless the comments may seem at the time. Her insecurity about her figure may not seem entirely rational, but that doesn't change her feelings, so be sensitive and reassuring.

> **"I made the big mistake of telling her I was worried she would let herself go and never get her figure back. She told me I was insensitive and felt she was being treated unfairly by my 'daddy insecurities'."**

How you feel about your pregnant wife's expanding middle can vary. You can be a little embarrassed because it's proof positive of what you've been doing with each other in private. You can be pleased and proud. You can silently worry that she may never look the same again.

During this time the mother of your unborn child will look for signs and reassurance that you're as thrilled about the baby as she is. She wants to talk about the baby and have you feel him move and kick. If you fail to show sufficient interest in those activities, she may feel that you don't love her or really want the baby. Her insecurity can seem extreme at times, but it goes with the territory.

> **"The best part of pregnancy is knowing there is a real little person growing inside my wife and feeling her move around."**
>
> **"My wife knew exactly what was going on with the baby at every stage of pregnancy. She was angry because she felt I didn't have the same interest."**

Part of your adjustment finds you retreating into your own emotional closet. This is the time you think about what kind of a dad you want to be. You think about your own father and the relationship you had, or wished you had, with him. Sometime during the second trimester most men plunge headlong into their impending fatherhood. You start spending more time with your married friends who have kids. You spend more time noticing children and their actions. Your emotions lurch from high hopes to high anxiety about your coming fatherhood role. It can help to talk to your male friends who have children and will understand your feelings. Look for an expectant father support group in your community. Share your concerns and fears. Refer to Chapter 9 "Prepared Parenting."

> **"The worst part of pregnancy has been the extra financial responsibilities, even though we planned for this, and worrying about day-care availability."**

This is also a good time to start emotionally connecting with your baby in a tangible way. Since babies are able to hear in utero, start talking or even singing to this developing baby of yours and let him know that you're his dad and you love him already. Give him the opportunity to become accustomed to your voice. Don't be surprised if he recognizes it after his birth. Think of it as another bonding tool. It's never too early to set the stage for the kind of relationship you hope to have with your child.

> **"I sang to my son all during pregnancy. The first time I held him, I sang to him—I swear he recognized my voice."**

Third Trimester—Anticipation

The third trimester finds both you and your wife in a state of anticipation. She's more serene and content to let you handle things like the national debt, foreign trade, and what to have for dinner. She has become "earth mother," and her nesting instinct is in full force those last few weeks. She'll look at the nursery a dozen times a day, clean out closets, scrub floors, and rearrange furniture. She's determined that everything will be just perfect for this little stranger who'll be your houseguest for the next 18 or so years. Her passivity and heightened vulnerability can make you feel very protective toward her.

> **"She has become more emotionally dependent on me. I have become even more protective of her and the baby."**

During this time, your earlier fears about childbirth and your concern for your wife and baby may resurface. You're more amenable if not eager to take childbirth classes with your wife as you start training for your role as coach now that the big event draws near. You want to feel the baby move. You paint the nursery and think about names. You are ready and eager to be a daddy to this little stranger who has a great time using his mom's stomach as a punching bag and trampoline.

CARING COMMUNICATION

Expectant mothers are naturally and normally rather obsessed with their pregnancy. It's often difficult for most men to share the same degree of involvement. It's common for expectant fathers to feel neglected, left out, and misunderstood at times. Its not that your wife makes you feel that way intentionally; she gets a little off-center and doesn't realize it.

> **"To say she was self-involved is a euphemism. She read every book she could find. She was always asking me to feel the baby move. The first time it was exciting, by the 200th time, I'd had enough. My lack of enthusiasm upset her.**

If you feel left out and neglected and start becoming irritated when she wants to talk about the baby—which may seem like all the time—that's your signal to gently remind her that it's time to nurture your "coupleness." Your relationship with each other is still just as important as the one you'll have with your baby; one shouldn't take a backseat to the other. This thought is especially important after the baby comes. You really have to pay attention to and work at keeping the intimacy and romance alive in your relationship in order to maintain your sense of coupleness. With this approach, she's more likely to be responsive to your feelings and less likely to mistakenly think you're insensitive and uncaring.

The voyage to parenthood isn't always smooth sailing. Your relationship has to weather a number of shifts and changes. Most of the problems couples encounter during pregnancy can be traced to either lack of communication or miscommunication. Pregnancy tests the quality of the communication styles you've developed and used over your time together as a couple. If your communication patterns with each other have not served you well in the past, pay particular attention to Chapter 9 and check the Recommended Resources for some books that will help you talk to each other and resolve issues in more effective ways. This is not the time in your relationship to ignore things or close your eyes, hoping to survive any storms you encounter. You both need to be acutely aware of and plan for any potential problems along the way to avoid your love boat running aground. For instance—

Be aware of where you are in relation to those developmental tasks you both have to work through. If your wife has worked through that first task of accepting the reality of the pregnancy, and you're still stuck dealing with ambivalence, it won't be a fun time for either one of you. If you can't resolve issues on your own, get some help.

Talk to each other—and really listen. This is an intensely emotional time for most couples. Pay attention to your feelings, needs, and concerns. Don't let things slide. Communicate your feelings to your wife. Encourage her to do the same. You need to be there for each other.

> **"Since pregnancy, the quality of our communication is sometimes greater, and sometimes total misconception."**
>
> **"She's always there for me."**

If you find that you're stuck in that ambivalence stage and having trouble bridging the gap emotionally to fatherhood, get some help. Many communities have organized support groups for new and expectant fathers. Check it out. This is a very important time for both of you. Your relationship is changing and growing. You want the changes to be healthy, just like your baby.

ΔΔΔ

2

SEXUALITY

Feast or famine

This chapter is an overview of the range of feelings and adaptations couples have and make in their sexual relationship during pregnancy. Whether you find yourself in the middle of or at opposite ends of the sexual spectrum matters not. Avoiding the pitfalls and emerging from pregnancy with an even greater emotional and sexual intimacy as a couple do matter. How well you weather these changes in your sexual relationship depends greatly on how well you communicate and support each other from the beginning. Couples who are able to share their fears and feelings in constructive ways report a heightened intimacy during pregnancy that adds a new dimension to their relationship, both emotionally and sexually.

There is great diversity in the sexual adaptation of couples during pregnancy. The changing physical and emotional factors complicate the adjustment process and causes confusion for many couples, which isn't surprising since both husband and wife are undergoing tremendous emotional growth in their transition from couple to family. The physical changes of pregnancy add another variable for both spouses. The pregnant woman has to deal with her own feelings about her changing body, while many a man finds their libido affected by his wife's "new look." It's enough to derail even the healthiest sex life.

> **"Our sexual relationship ended with pregnancy. My sex drive didn't react well to my wife's pregnant body. I became a practicing celibate."**

The First 3 Months

In the first 3 months, your sex drive may shift into low gear. The tales of childbirth you may have heard could make you fearful for your wife. The fear can produce a guilty feeling because of what you "did to her." The feeling isn't rational, but it's normal. You also worry that you might hurt the baby during intercourse. Fear not—routine sex is safe during pregnancy.

> **"Our sex frequency is much less."**
>
> **"Even though she was pretty fatigued, our sex life was more spontaneous since we didn't have to worry about birth control."**

The fun and closeness you shared before pregnancy can seem like a dream in those early weeks. This is a very important time to set the tone for the rest of the pregnancy. You both need understanding and support. Now is the time to put into practice the caring communication that will help you both avoid the misunderstandings that will continue to surface even after pregnancy is long over. Anger and resentments don't disappear; they hang around to haunt you later. Showing your concern and kindness now pays dividends in the second and third trimesters.

> **"With pregnancy, our sex life was not as free and carefree, and lustful."**

Mostly what you'll face will be the loss of your wife's libido. Her nipples are sore. She's tired, irritable, and moody, and she may be sick a great deal of the time. In fact, she may be spending more time hugging the toilet bowl than you. Nausea is not a known aphrodisiac; even if you looked like her favorite movie star, she wouldn't be interested. Don't take it personally; this is only a temporary inconvenience, not a life-long sentence to celibacy. Before you know it, her nipples won't be sore, and the fatigue and morning sickness will disappear. You'll be relieved to see that glint back in her eye when she looks at you.

The Second Trimester

During the second trimester, famine turns into feast for many couples. Your wife is energized. She feels great. Her body hasn't outgrown her libido yet, and she wants your body! During this part of pregnancy, women commonly have sexual fantasies. The female organs are perfused with extra blood because of pregnancy changes this engorgement encourages romantic and lustful thoughts. You may both be delighted with her enlarged breast size, and she may find breast stimulation even more erotic than before. It's not unusual for a woman to experience her first orgasm or have heightened orgasms during this time. If your sex drive is still intact, you wonder if this is heaven. Memorize this wonderful time. You'll need it for the last few months of pregnancy.

> **"I was attracted to my wife just as much, if not more, there was a specialness about her—that glow of pregnancy"**

The Third Trimester

Remember the lustful fires of desire that crackled between you in the previous months? They're now flickering embers of faded ecstasy. Your love boat has run aground. What was familiar territory has now become increasingly foreign. Your wife is feeling more like a lumbering bear heading for hibernation than the sex goddess you knew in the second trimester. You may find your sex drive on hold for any number of reasons. This woman who used to start forest fires in your southern region just doesn't look the same. She looks, well, motherly. You may find yourself looking at her differently. Don't worry. It's common to have those Oedipal feelings resurface. Your psyche is trying to reconcile your changing perceptions of yourself in relation to your wife and your imminent role of father. It can be definitely confusing and disconcerting at times.

By the end of this trimester, most couples report a decrease in both interest and frequency of intercourse. You find your creativity being stretched to the limit in trying to find new positions that make sex possible. When you seek some creative consultation by asking "How shall we do this?" her answer is likely to be "As quickly as possible!" Try not to take her response too personally. Her sexual organs are chronically engorged now, and even orgasm doesn't bring total relief. Orgasm can cause uterine contractions, which can be a little scary for you both. Don't worry. The contractions are a little uncomfortable, but they don't cause any harm. Nipple stimulation produces the same result. The "missionary" position is just a memory. The other possible positions provide deep penetration that can be painful. Your choices are limited to vaginal entry from the side or rear in the spoon position. "We Shall Overcome" is your new theme song.

> **"We didn't know orgasm could cause contractions. We were very worried when it happened."**
>
> **"Sex became nonexistent by the 7th month."**

At times you'll need to feel a greater closeness with your wife. Your "daddy insecurities" can get the best of you. These are the times you feel insecure about the coming changes and of emotionally losing her to the new baby. You may feel the need to make love as a way to comfort and reassure you at times like these. Tell her how you feel and what you need. She'll love it.

> **"We have sex less frequently, especially during the third trimester due to lack of comfortable positions— although we are closer emotionally."**

Even though there will be times when your wife may not be interested in the physical act of love, she craves closeness, affection, and comfort from you. If you're conditioned to the idea that physical affection always proceeds to sex, the potential for disappointment for you both is high. If ever there was a time to be very sensitive of each other's needs, now is it. Talk to each other! Listen when she shares her feelings with you. You're in this together. If you decide to forgo intercourse for the rest of the pregnancy, try not to think of it as deprivation; think of it as a time to expand the horizons of your sexual and emotional intimacy. See it as a fun challenge; be inventive and creative. Explore new pathways of eroticism and intimacy that don't include intercourse. See it as an opportunity at best and a temporary inconvenience at worst.

> **"We focused less on sex and more on the baby."**
>
> **"We have developed a greater nonsexual intimacy."**

General Rules

Very few sexual practices have to be avoided during pregnancy. The list isn't long. Blowing air into the vagina can cause an air embolism that could prove fatal during pregnancy. While a vibrator used externally for clitoral stimulation is safe, rigid vibrators inserted into the vagina can cause bleeding and possible damage to the cervix. If you have any questions or concerns, ask your doctor. Try not to be shy or embarrassed because your doctor has heard it all. An excellent book that deals with sex in pregnancy is *Making Love During Pregnancy* by Bing and Coleman. See the Recomended Resources in Appendix 1.

A big question for most couples is when to stop having intercourse. Very few if any doctors still recommend abstaining from sex for 6 weeks before delivery. Usually, you can continue until the water breaks. If the pregnancy remains normal, there's no reason why you can't make the decision yourselves. You'll find her physical changes a prime factor in whether or when you decide to give up sex for the duration.

> **"My sex drive didn't diminish at all. The discomfort on my wife's part actually was the limiting factor."**

A simple rule to follow is, if it still feels good to her, enjoy yourselves. Cultivate your patience and a healthy sense of humor to help you cope and keep your perspective. This is all part of the growing experience for your relationship.

> **"Sexually, in the last trimester, it brought new meaning to the word flexibility."**

ΔΔΔ

3

MONTHS, MILESTONES, AND MISERIES

THE DUE DATE

Pregnancy usually lasts 265 days from conception, or 280 days from the first day of the last menses, assuming a 28-day cycle. The doctor calculates in terms of lunar months of 28 days as opposed to calendar months of 31 days. Consequently, pregnancy lasts 10 lunar months (40 weeks) or 9 calendar months. Since the majority of health care workers refer to pregnancy only in terms of weeks, not lunar or calendar months, it's less confusing to get in the habit of thinking about weeks from the beginning.

About 50 percent of all pregnant women will deliver 1 week before the due date, and 1 in 10 will go 2 weeks beyond the due date. A due date is merely a ballpark figure, not an absolute. Remember this as the time draws near or passes by and you begin to think that pregnancy is forever.

MATERNAL MISERIES

The growth of your baby and the physiological changes in your wife's body go hand in hand to produce those aches and pains known as the common complaints that come and go during pregnancy. This section is an overview of the more common complaints your wife may experience and ways you may be able to help her with them. The aches and pains are discussed at the approximate point in pregnancy at which they usually occur. But because everyone's different, there's always variations as to when they occur and recur throughout pregnancy.

The most of those minor ailments are caused by the hormones of pregnancy, which soften ligaments and make joints more unstable. For instance, the normal increase in blood volume experienced early in pregnancy contributes to varicose veins and the swollen feet and ankles that may occur in the last trimester.

As the baby grows, the mother's center of gravity changes. The weight of her growing uterus pulls her forward, which stresses and strains the lower back and leg muscles. Think about how uncomfortable you'd be carrying a 25 pound pack strapped to your middle all day and you get a fairly good idea of how your pregnant wife feels. The following table is the breakdown of how the extra weight is distributed.

AVERAGE WEIGHT OF PRODUCTS OF PREGNANCY

Component	Pounds
Baby	7.5
Placenta	1.0
Amniotic fluid	2.0
Uterus, weight increase	2.5
Breast tissue, weight increase	3.0
Blood volume increase	4.0
Maternal fat stores	4.0 to 8.0
Total	24.0 to 28.0

4 TO 8 WEEKS
Baby

Your baby is still considered an embryo during the first 8 weeks and measures about 1-1/2 inches (4 centimeters) in size. The heart is the most developed organ at this point. The arms and legs are still buds, and the umbilical cord is beginning to form. In the early weeks, a fetus more closely resembles a miniature Klingon from Star Trek than a human baby. The various bodily parts appear and develop at different rates until the sixteenth week, when all the parts catch up with each other and finally resemble a regular baby you'd recognize. Some couples find it disconcerting to see real pictures of babies before they're fully developed. If you're interested in the real thing, check the Recommended Resources.

Mom

In the first trimester of pregnancy, your wife's body is making a number of adjustments. She's bombarded by the hormones of pregnancy, which produce the first common complaints.

During this time her breasts enlarge, and her nipples and surrounding skin (areola) turn from pink to brown. She may experience headaches.

■ Helpful Hints

During this first trimester, your wife shouldn't take any medications without consulting her doctor. After the first trimester, when the baby is completely formed, Tylenol is safe for minor aches and pains such as headaches.

Have her lie down in a darkened, quiet room and apply a wet, cold cloth to her forehead. Rub her feet and apply firm but gentle pressure to areas on and around her big toes; the acupressure site for headaches. It may help or at least distract her from her headache.

During these early weeks, the pregnant woman is more susceptible to low blood sugar because she's transporting sugar from her blood through the placenta to nourish the baby. It's common for women to feel faint and dizzy, especially if they've skipped meals.

Nausea, commonly known as morning sickness, may appear about the sixth week of pregnancy. It can strike at any time of the day or night, which makes it difficult for her to keep food on her stomach.

On top of everything else, she's definitely tired. The fatigue she experiences is all-consuming. She may not be able or want to do anything but sleep in her spare time. In spite of the fatigue, some women also have insomnia, which isn't a good combination.

■ Helpful Hints

Encourage your wife to eat small meals throughout the day to avoid low blood sugar.

Before bedtime, a carbohydrate/protein snack such as milk or an apple may help prevent low blood sugar in the morning. Keep crackers by her bedside so she can nibble on them before she gets up. Take over cooking breakfast in the morning, and avoid cooking foods that may aggravate her nausea. For example, some women can't tolerate the smell of bacon frying, but everyone's different. A "milkshake" made of fruit yogurt, banana, and a little low-fat milk might appeal to her. You'll have to experiment.

Support your wife's need to get the extra rest and sleep she needs during this time. It's only a temporary condition, so do what you can to help her; she will truly appreciate your pitching in when she really needs you. If you're married to superwoman, try to help her control herself before she drops from exhaustion trying to maintain her high level of activity.

If she has insomnia, advise her to eliminate her intake of caffeine for a few days. Pregnant women don't metabolize caffeine very efficiently, and it may contribute to her insomnia.

12 TO 16 WEEKS
Baby

This is the stage when an ultrasound exam might be done. Between 12 and 16 weeks, your baby is about 3 inches in size and weighs only 1/4 of a pound (110 grams). Arm and leg buds have blossomed, and nails are developing. Fine hair begins to appear on the body, and sexual development is apparent. Her skin is very transparent. The heartbeat can now be heard with an ultrasound stethoscope.

Mom

By now her body has adjusted to early pregnancy. Her nausea, fatigue, and sore breasts are gone. She feels wonderful and begins to display that glow of pregnancy. Between now and 24 weeks she won't have a lot to complain about.

20 WEEKS
Baby

Your baby now weighs a little under 1 pound (300 grams) and has fine silky hair (lanugo) all over her body. Hair on the head is beginning to sprout. This is the halfway point in the pregnancy. You can feel little kicks and movements. This is a good time to start talking to your baby, if you haven't already. Read her your favorite fairy tales from childhood, introduce her to Dr. Seuss, and tell her about the family waiting for her—siblings, aunts, uncles, and grandparents. Play music for her. Babies seem to prefer peaceful music so forget heavy metal and go for Mozart.

Mom

Your wife's uterus has reached her navel. This is usually a nice time for a woman during pregnancy. She can now wear maternity clothes that leave no doubt she's pregnant. She's proud of her pregnancy figure and delights in feeling the baby move. She has few, if any, aches and pains during this time.

24 WEEKS
Baby

At 6 lunar months, the average weight of a baby is 1-1/2 pounds (630 grams). Her skin is wrinkled, but fat deposits are forming and in time will smooth things out. The head is noticeably larger than the body. Eyebrows and lashes are present.

Babies born at this time may be able to breathe briefly, but they're still not ready for the outside world.

Mom

Mild complaints may begin to appear at this time. The hormones of pregnancy slow down bowel function so maximum absorption of vitamins and nutrients can occur. The increasing weight of the growing uterus contributes to constipation.

False contractions, known as Braxton-Hick's contractions can be noticed now. (The uterus actually contracts all during pregnancy but the sensation isn't felt until about this time.) The uterus exercises its muscle to keep in shape for labor and delivery. These contractions are mild and not painful; seeming more like the baby rolling into a ball.

Some women's feet and ankles begin to swell at the end of the day. This is a benign condition caused by the increase in blood volume and the weight of the growing uterus on large vessels, which traps fluid in the lower extremities.

■ Helpful Hints

Alleviate constipation by adding 2 or 3 tablespoons of unprocessed bran to your wife's diet, either to cereal or mixing it with milk or juice each morning. Keep adding an extra tablespoon each morning until she gets results. Using laxatives isn't recommended because her bowel will get used to the harsh stimulation and in time won't function without its "fix."

There's a very simple solution for swollen feet and ankles. If she finds swelling a problem, she can lie on her left side for 20 minutes each day, which will relieve the pressure on the large vessels to reabsorb fluid back into her system.

Precaution

There's no need to take water pills to relieve the swelling. Doctors no longer recommend their use; the pills can upset the chemical balance in a pregnant woman's body. Excess fluid isn't the problem, merely misplaced fluid. Salt restriction isn't recommended either. Normal amounts of salt should remain in your wife's diet. If she has questions or concerns about her swelling, she should discuss them with her doctor.

28 WEEKS
Baby

Your little sweetheart now weighs a little over 2 pounds and is 16 inches long. The skin is red and covered with nature's "cold cream," called vernix caseosa. With expert care in a sophisticated neonatal intensive care unit, most babies born at this point survive.

Mom

Now that the baby is getting bigger, more strain is put on your wife's lower back and calf muscles. She may begin experiencing leg cramps and restless legs at night. It's difficult to suffer silently, so she'll wake you up too if a cramp strikes. Restless legs will keep you both awake. Her legs will seem to have a life of their own as they twitch and jump, no matter how hard she tries to control them.

Varicose veins in her legs and vaginal area may appear also from the increased weight on the blood vessels. She is definitely feeling pregnant by now.

■ Helpful Hints

Prevent leg cramps and restless legs by relaxing and stretching her calf muscles before she retires for the night. A warm bath loosens those tired muscles. To stretch the muscles, have her stand 2 feet away from the wall with her hands about eye level. She should extend one leg behind her and keep her knee straight. The heels of her feet should remain flat on the floor as she leans forward until she feels the stretch in the backs of her legs. She should hold the stretch for 20 to 30 seconds. The stretch should be gentle and steady stretch, not bouncy. She can repeat the stretch until she no longer feels any tension in her calves.

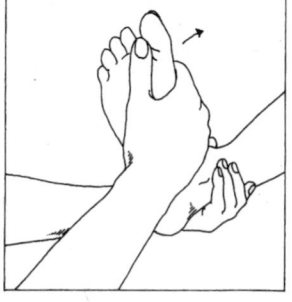

If a leg cramp strikes, push the ball of her foot toward her knees. Exert steady pressure for about 1 minute; if you let up too soon, the cramp will recur.

Varicose veins can be helped but probably not eliminated by avoiding constipation. Your wife should also avoid sitting or standing for long stretches. Luckily, after delivery of the baby, the problems resolves itself.

32 WEEKS
Baby

At 8 lunar months you can relax because babies born at this time have an excellent survival rate. Their average weight is around 4 pounds (1800 grams).

Mom

At this stage of the game, your wife will probably be whisking you off to prepared childbirth classes. She will also be intent on picking names and finding the right crib.

Her lower back may bother her now. Most women have varying degrees of back pain during pregnancy. Many women add heartburn, hemorrhoids, and round ligament pain to their growing list of complaints. After the fifth month, round ligament pain comes and goes. The round ligaments that hold up the uterus soften and stretch easily in pregnancy. As the weight increases, so does the strain on the ligaments. Your wife may tell you she feels as if her bottom is falling out. The pain can come and go or last for days at a time. It can be extremely uncomfortable, but it's benign.

■ Helpful Hints

Good body mechanics help avoid aggravating lower back symptoms. Help her remember to lift with her legs, not her back; hold objects close to her body: and lift objects only chest high.

Your wife can move her car seat forward to keep her knees bent and higher than her hips. A small pillow helps support the lower back also.

Sensible shoes are a must during pregnancy. Heels more than 1 inch high only add to lower back strain.

The following exercise helps rest and stretch lower back muscles: Using the back of a chair for support and balance, she should assume a squatting position for a 30-second interval and then rest for 15 seconds. Repeat this exercise at least 6 times, 6 times a day.

Heartburn can be alleviated but not eliminated until the baby is born. Avoiding large or unusually spicy meals before bedtime and taking antacids like Tums and Amphogel often help. Sleeping in a semipropped position with 2 or 3 pillows brings some relief.

Hemorrhoids are aggravated by constipation, so as much fiber as possible should be included in the pregnant woman's diet. Treat pain and swelling with warm soaks and local anesthetic agents sold over the counter.

You can help relieve your wife's round ligament pain somewhat by her lying on the bed while you grasp her ankles and then bend her knees and elevate her hips off the bed. Doing this "wheelbarrow" exercise several times a day helps relieve the pressure of the stretched ligaments.

36 WEEKS
Baby

A baby at this stage is 16 to18 inches long and about 5 1/2 pounds. Her wrinkles are almost gone, and your little ballerina is keeping your wife awake most nights doing twirls until 2 a.m.

Mom

The thrill of pregnancy is probably wearing thin for both of you. Your wife may have numerous recurring complaints, and the list is growing daily. At this time it's common for her to feel dizzy or faint if she stands in one place too long, such as waiting in the grocery line. When she doesn't move around, blood pools in her lower extremities. Her blood pressure drops, and she gets dizzy and may even faint.

Remind her to move her legs around if she has to stand in one place for a few minutes. If she faints, be sure to turn her to her side so her uterus doesn't cut off the blood supply from her large vessels (the vena cava syndrome). Her blood pressure can drop even lower and cut off oxygen to the baby which is why she shouldn't lie on her back after the fifth month.

40 WEEKS

Baby

Your baby nows weighs between 6 and 9 pounds. It's very crowded in there. You're amazed at how elastic a body can be as she looks more and more like the mom who devoured Brooklyn.

Mom

The baby is now sitting on top of his mom's bladder. She'll be spending most of her time in the bathroom. At night she'll have to get up several times to empty her bladder. Between the baby and her bladder, she won't be getting much quality sleep.

She may have nightmares and bizarre dreams at this time. Many women dream they have puppies instead of a baby or had a baby but lost him somewhere. They also dream about labor and delivery.

Your wife is sick of being pregnant. Mother Nature's very wise: She makes women so miserable that they think even labor and delivery are preferable to being pregnant. You're both ready to get this over with.

ΔΔΔ

4

HEALTHY HABITS

Pregnancy is an ideal time for both you and your wife to evaluate your health habits and make important changes. If you continue to drink alcohol and/or smoke during her pregnancy, it makes it more difficult for her to avoid them. If you're going to set an example for your wife and be a good role model for your child, you need to start now.

Pregnancy is a highly impressionable time in a woman's life. She's especially vulnerable to well-meaning advice. Everyone wants to have a healthy baby, but the burning desire to do "all the right things" can cause unnecessary feelings of fear and guilt. You can help your wife be more objective about the advice she incorporates into her daily regimen.

NUTRITION

Nutrition, one of the sacred cows in pregnancy, is a commonly misunderstood topic. Some books claim to have magic dietary formulas for pregnancy that guarantee to ward off preeclampsia and preterm labor and guarantee you a healthy baby. However, there are no known diets that will produce those results. The standard is still a well-balanced diet—nothing complicated or magical. A diet that includes 20 percent protein, 30 percent or less fats, and 50 percent carbohydrates will give a pregnant woman energy, a sense of well-being, and adequate calories for her baby. The most important nutritional priority in pregnancy, as it relates to the baby, is simply ingesting adequate calories (approximately 2200-2400) per day.

In the first trimester of pregnancy, your wife may have a difficult time meeting the daily requirements due to nausea or decreased appetite. Don't worry; the baby won't suffer any ill effects.

The following is a sample of a 1 day well-balanced diet that provides all the right components of carbohydrates, proteins, fats, and calcium.

SAMPLE MENU

Food group		Calories	Carb. (gm)	Prot. (gm)	Fat (gm)	Calcium (mgm)
	Breakfast					
1 cereal	3/4 cup Wheat chex	100	23	3	0	12
	2 tsp. sugar	32	8	0	0	0
1 dairy	1 cup low fat milk	120	12	8	5	300
1 fruit	1 small orange	60	15	1	0	50
	Snack					
2 fruit	**1** banana	105	23	2	0	0
	Lunch					
2 bread	2 slices whole wheat	120	22	6	2	60
1 fat	2 tsp. mayonnaise	67	0	0	7	0
1 meat	1 oz. turkey breast	60	0	7	3	3
1 vegetable	1 oz. romaine lettuce	9	2	1		20
2 fruit	1 cup V-8 juice	50	10	2	0	30
1 bread	8 Wheat thins	70	9	1	3	0

SAMPLE MENU (CONTINUED)

Snack						
1 milk	cottage cheese					
	1/2 cup	100	4	16	3	78
1 fruit	raisins 1/3 cup	150	40	1	0	25
	Dinner					
3 meat	3 oz. baked					
	chicken	165	0	21	9	0
1 vegetable	Baked potato	145	39	8	0	8
2 fat	1 tsp. butter/					
	margarine	36	0	0	4	1
	1 oz. low-fat					
	plain yogurt	18	2	1	0	51
2 vegetable	1/2 cup peas	67	12	4	0	22
1 vegetable	Salad with romaine					
	lettuce and 1/2 cup					
	tomatoes	33	6	2	0	28
4 fat	salad dressing					
	4 tbs. (oil/vinegar)	290	0	0	32	0
1 dairy	1 cup low-fat milk	120	12	18	5	300
	Snack					
1 bread	1 slice French bread	80	13	3	1	22
1 fat	1 tsp. peanut butter	95	3	5	8	5
1 milk	8 z. low-fat milk	120	12	8	5	300
	Total	2212	262	108	87	1322
			57%	24%	20%	

If you would both like to improve your eating habits, call a registered dietician for a consultation; it's a worthwhile investment. Do a 48 hour diet recall to take with you.

WEIGHT GAIN

The Committee on Nutritional Status During Pregnancy recommends adequate calories that result in a maternal weight gain of 25 to 30 pound, to produce healthier babies who are less likely to have problems.

How Much?

A woman usually gains 2 to 4 pounds in the first 12 weeks, depending on the severity of her nausea. After that, she'll gain 1 pound a week for the last 28 weeks of pregnancy. After the first trimester, a weight gain of less than 1/2 pound in a month is too little, and more than 6 1/2 pounds in a month is too much. If she is overweight, she should still gain 15 to 25 pounds; pregnancy is no time to lose weight. A weight gain of less than 15 pounds for overweight women produces a mortality rate twice that of those overweight women who gain the recommended weight.

The last 3 months is an especially important time for women to gain weight since the baby is growing rapidly at this time. Those brain cells that will make her the next Einstein need all the nourishment they can get.

VITAMINS AND MINERALS

Experts claim vitamin supplements aren't necessary in pregnancy. Ask the experts if they prescribe prenatal vitamins for their patients—they do. Old habits are hard to break. If your wife decides to take prenatal vitamins, remind her that they aren't a substitute for food. Megavitamin therapy should definitely be avoided because some vitamins in large doses can cause birth defects. Extra iron is usually needed and prescribed during pregnancy.

Calcium is an important component of a healthy diet. Both your wife and baby benefit from a calcium intake of 1200 milligrams per day. Your baby needs it for bone and teeth development, and your wife needs it to replenish her own stores of calcium so she can avoid osteoporosis (softening of the bones) in later life. The best source of calcium comes from dairy products. Four 8-ounce glasses of milk per day provide the needed amounts of calcium. If your wife has a milk intolerance and experiences bloating and gas, buy her milk that has the lactose removed, or try yogurt, which is also high in calcium.

Salt should not be restricted during pregnancy; it doesn't cause toxemia. Moderate use of salt should be continued, while avoiding overindulgence in potato chips and other excessively salty foods.

DRUGS
Prescription and Over-the-Counter Drugs

During pregnancy, especially **the first 3 months, your wife should avoid all drugs except those prescribed by her doctor.** The placenta acts like a sieve, not a barrier, and most substances pass through to the baby. To have a problem such as a birth defect from a drug, the right combination of circumstances has to be in effect: The baby has to be at a certain point developmentally combined with a special susceptibility to a particular drug. It's like playing Russian Roulette. Your chances of missing the bullet are pretty good, but you never know until it's too late. Pregnancy normally carries a 2 to 4 percent risk for abnormalities. Drugs are implicated in approximately 6 percent of birth defects. The risk for problems is real, but small.

By the second trimester, the only over-the-counter drugs worth using are Tylenol for headaches and Tums for heartburn. Anything else, such as cold remedies, are basically useless. Laxatives can be avoided by adding bran to cereal in the morning. Diuretics (water pills) should be avoided, period. Swollen ankles and feet at the end of the day are a common occurrence in pregnancy and no cause for alarm. If your wife's face and hands are swollen also, she needs to call her doctor because generalized swelling can be a sign of toxemia and needs medical attention. See Chapter 10 "Potential Problems."

Social/Recreational Drugs
Alcohol

Social drugs should be avoided. The exact amount of alcohol it takes to produce adverse effects on the baby is unknown, but 3 or more ounces of alcohol per day puts your baby in the high-risk category for problems. Alcohol passes right through the placenta. If your wife is tipsy, so is your baby. You wouldn't dream of giving alcohol to your newborn baby, so don't give it to your unborn baby either.

Nicotine

Smoking causes blood vessels to constrict, decreasing the blood flow that carries nutrients and oxygen to your baby. Smoking also inhibits the absorption of calcium and vitamin C—your wife ends up with wrinkles and soft bones. Help her kick her habit, especially during pregnancy. If you smoke too, consider quitting with her. The dangers of second-hand smoke now affect your baby too. Children of parents who smoke continue to show a decrease in their lung function as they grow older, and experience more respiratory problems such as colds and coughs.

Cocaine

Recreational drugs such as cocaine are anything but fun to your baby. The drug decreases blood flow to the placenta, causing a temporary but dramatic drop in oxygen available to the baby. The severe pressure from the vasoconstriction can tear the placenta away from the uterine wall, causing an obstetrical hemorrhage that endangers both your wife and baby. Studies now suggest that babies born to mothers who use cocaine have permanent neurological problems in addition to experiencing withdrawal after birth. If your wife uses cocaine, she has a major problem that will affect the health and well-being of your child. Insist she get help.

Marijuana

Pot has been many things to many cultures over the centuries. The Chinese discovered it 5000 years ago and used it as a healing herb. The British in the 1800s considered it a wonder drug and used it as a cure-all. Muslims used it for everything from asthma to dandruff, and George Washington made ropes out of it.

There's a temptation in light of the current drug crisis to minimize the dangers of pot. Compared to crack cocaine it seems like a quaint and relatively harmless recreational pursuit, but it's not.

For the pregnant woman, marijuana's effects are the same as cigarette smoking. Women who smoke marijuana during pregnancy have a fivefold increase in the probability of delivering a baby with fetal alcohol syndrome (FAS) features. There's a greater incidence of miscarriage, low birthweight babies, stillbirth, and neonatal deaths. Insist your wife find a safer, healthier way to get high. Exercise or meditation are good substitutes.

EXERCISE

In a normal pregnancy, a well-established exercise program can be continued without problems. Researchers have found that even though blood is shunted away from the uterus during strenuous exercise, the baby compensates quite well—no harm done. When a pregnancy develops a complication such as preeclampsia, which involves blood flow to the placenta, exercise isn't advised because the baby already has enough problems coping with decreased oxygen levels. See Chapter 10.

If your wife didn't exercise before pregnancy, now is no time to start training for the Boston Marathon. Exercise won't produce a faster or easier labor. Couch potatoes do as well as Olympic marathoners. If she wants to exercise safely during her pregnancy, share the following guidelines adapted from The American College of Obstetricians and Gynecologists.

General Guidelines

Fit or not, pregnancy brings some physical changes that alter your wife's ability to engage in physical activity. The hormones of pregnancy make her joints more unstable, and ligaments and tissues are more relaxed. Her center of gravity changes, especially as pregnancy advances. Her balance is more precarious. The chances of injury increase. She needs to make allowances for the changes.

Exercise can help to smooth out those emotional swings that pregnancy can bring by liberating mood-elevating endorphins. When she starts acting like Godzilla on a rampage, head her off at the pass: grab her hand and take a brisk walk together. You'll both feel better. It's also a great time to really talk to each other—no phones, TV, or other distractions.

Swimming is particularly safe and suited to pregnancy. Many health clubs offer aquafitness programs for their pregnant clientele. Your wife can maintain her aerobic fitness without worrying about injuries.

Bike riding is not really recommended for the pregnant woman, but a stationary bike is considered safe because she doesn't have to wear a helmet and she won't fall over. Just be sure she isn't overextending her knee and hip joints while pedaling. Remind her to check her pulse to avoid exceeding the 140 beats per minute limit.

If aerobic classes are her passion, she can continue to participate. Low impact aerobics are best suited to the pregnant woman. She should let her instructor know that she is pregnant, not try to keep up with her pregnant cohorts, and listen to her body. Some days she just won't have the energy.

EXERCISE GUIDELINES

PREGNANCY AND POSTPARTUM

Do

1. Regular exercise at least three times per week.

2. Precede vigorous exercise with a 5-minute period of muscle warm-up. Slow walking or stationary cycling with low resistance is effective.

3. Gradually decrease activity. For example, after fast walking, finish with very slow walking. Conclude with gentle stationary stretching. Make stretches slow and steady. Hold the stretch about for 20 seconds and relax into it. Avoid bouncy movements that snap muscles like rubber bands, which is how injuries occur.

4. Take your pulse during peak activity. Keep target heart rate within limits set by your physician. *Maternal heart rate should not exceed 140 beats per minute.* You need a watch with a second hand. If you count 23 beats in 10 seconds, you're within the limits. Athletic stores also sell devices that strap on your finger and give you a continuous recording of your pulse rate. In general, if you're able to carry on a conversation comfortably while exercising, your heart rate is probably within the recommended limits. Check to make sure.

5. Exercise on a wooden floor or a tightly carpeted surface to reduce shock and provide sure footing.

6. Rise gradually to avoid dizziness from floor-lying exercises. Periodically move your legs to keep your blood circulating.

7. Drink liquids before and after exercise to prevent dehydration. Replenish fluids as necessary.

8. Assure adequate caloric intake to meet both the extra energy needs of pregnancy and the exercise performed.

9. Consult your physician if any unusual symptoms occur during exercise.

EXERCISE GUIDELINES (CONTINUED)

Don't

1. Exercise in hot, humid weather or during any illness if you have a fever.

2. Engage in exercise that requires deep flexion or extension of joints, jumping, jarring motions, or rapid changes in direction. Don't use jerky, bouncy motions such as those used in racquetball, tennis, or high impact aerobics. However, If you're well conditioned and have been engaging in these sports previous to pregnancy, listen to your body. You'll know when you need to modify your exercise regimen.

PREGNANCY ONLY — Don't

1. Exercise strenuously for longer than 15 minutes.

2. Lie flat on your back after the fourth month of pregnancy has been completed.

3. Raise your core temperature more than 38° centigrade (100.4° Fahrenheit).

4. Use exercises that require you to hold your breath or bear down (Valsalva maneuver).

Weight training is becoming more popular with pregnant women. It's an effective way to strengthen and tone muscles. Light to moderate weights are recommended. Exercises that might stress her lower back or put pressure on her abdominal muscles must be avoided. Nautilus equipment is safer than free weights because it's more stable. If your wife is a beginner in weight training, it's wise for her to consult with someone who is experienced and knowledgeable so she can follow a safe program.

Stretch and relaxation exercise such as yoga can also tone and strengthen muscles while reducing stress. No special equipment is needed. Yoga is good preparation for childbirth; teaching concentration, persistence, and patience. See the Recommended Resources for a stretch and relax book that is based on yoga poses. Try the exercises with your wife.

SPORTS

Hazardous sports such as horseback riding should be avoided during pregnancy for safety sake. Both snow and water skiing are not a good idea no matter how proficient your wife may be. Water skiing can force water into her vagina causing a life-threatening embolism, which just isn't worth the risks involved.

TRAVEL

As a general rule, traveling until the last month of pregnancy is considered safe. **Insist your wife wear her 3-point restraint seat belt.** Interrupt long trips for hourly pit stops so she can walk around and get her circulation going again. Pregnant women are especially susceptible to blood clots from sitting too long. If there's room, she can lie down in the back seat on her side to rest.

WORK

As long as pregnancy remains uncomplicated, your wife can continue to work until her due date if she so desires. If she's a bomb squad technician or a lumberjack, she may have to transfer to a less stressful and/or physically demanding job until she delivers.

If she works at a video display terminal (computer) there's no cause to worry it will harm the pregnancy because the initial concerns about low frequency magnetic fields and ultraviolet radiation have been discounted. It's recommended that a woman take 15-minute break from the computer every 2 hours so she can improve her circulation, and reduce eye and back strain.

PARTING ADVICE

Encourage your wife's desire to follow a healthier life style. Discourage adopting radical and/or rigid rules advocated by faddists of any type. For the most part, moderation in all things combined with common sense is a good creed to follow in pregnancy.

ΔΔΔ

PART 2

DEVELOPMENT
AND
PLANNING

5

PROCEDURES AND PURCHASES

In the course of becoming parents, you and your wife will have to make some decisions regarding feeding, foreskins, cribs, car seats, doctors, and diapers, to name but a few. Here are the pros and cons to help you make informed decisions that will work best for you.

BREAST-FEEDING

Some women have a deep emotional need to experience breast-feeding their baby, while others think that the whole idea is vastly overrated and have no desire to even try it. It's very important for you as a couple to be very clear on how you feel individually about breast-feeding before making a decision. Consider the following advantages and disadvantages.

Advantages

There's no debating that breast milk is the best source of food for a baby. It's also very convenient, attractively packaged, and free. The health advantages are:

- Colostrum (early milk) provides immunity factors for baby.
- Decreases the incidence of allergies; gastrointestinal ailments such as gas, colic, constipation, and diarrhea; respiratory problems; asthma; bronchitis; croup; colds; and other contagious diseases.
- Easily digestible, and baby is able to utilize all the components in the milk.
- Provides all necessary vitamins and minerals.
- Baby requires no other food until he's 6 months old.
- Makes baby less prone to obesity.

Disadvantages

- Gives the nursing mom less mobility, particularly in the first 6 weeks. Her breasts become full and very uncomfortable if they aren't emptied on time.
- Until mom's milk supply is well established, her breasts may leak, so she has to wear pads in her bra.
- Nursing takes longer than bottle-feeding, and breast-fed babies eat more often.
- Fatigue is a big problem until sleeping and feeding schedules are established.
- Occasionally, breast infections require antibiotics, but it's easily treated and nursing isn't interrupted.

The percentage of women breast-feeding their babies has been slowly declining in recent years. It's not clear why there's a downward trend, but possibly it has to do with the larger numbers of women who work outside the home. The task of breast pumping and/or being available to feed the baby may be too daunting a task for many women.

Some men find it very difficult to think of breasts as serving 2 functions: sexual and nutritional. If you see your wife's breasts as strictly sexual and your own personal erogenous zones, you may not be willing to share them with even your own baby. There's no problem if your wife shares your views and isn't eager to breast-feed. Problems surface when one partner is very committed to breast-feeding but the other one isn't.

It's common for the expectant father to worry about being left out emotionally by his wife's breast-feeding their baby. You may have doubts about how you feel. On one hand, you want your baby to have the best food possible, but you'd like to feed her too. It's important to keep in mind that there's more to nurturing your baby than feeding her. There are lots of other things you can do to help, such as changing diapers, and bathing, massaging, and rocking your baby. After the first 6 weeks, when your wife's milk supply is well established, she can pump her breasts so you can feed the baby too on those occasions when she goes shopping or just wants to get away for a few hours.

If you have a hard time resolving your feelings about your wife nursing your baby, remember that it isn't forever. The 6 months or so will go by quickly, and she'll appreciate your support for something that's very important to her. Taking the high road is preferable to sabotaging the process by being critical and non supportive.

Nursing and Sexuality

How is nursing going to affect your relationship as a couple, particularly the sexual aspect? There are some benefits to breast-feeding other than nutritional ones. For instance, women who nurse their babies are generally more eager to resume lovemaking (perhaps from the frequent nipple stimulation from nursing). Some women report that their sex drive is stronger than ever and orgasms better. Be forewarned: your wife's breasts may squirt milk with orgasm. You can think of this as an inconvenience, a delight, or a validation of orgasm. Nursing breasts aren't off-limits for sex; you and your baby can share them if you wish.

While some women are more sexual with nursing, others are less so. Some women become tired of the constant demand on their bodies, and some want time-out for themselves, becoming less inclined to resume lovemaking.

Most men find that the quality and frequency of sex correlate directly with how much help and support they give their wives. When you help your wife with the housework and the baby, you're building a solid foundation for the nurturing relationship you want with your new baby and strengthening the one you already have with your wife. It's an unbeatable combination.

Obstacles to Success

Breast-feeding isn't an instinctual process for either baby or mom; it has to be learned. If you aren't in favor of your wife breast-feeding your baby, you present a formidable obstacle to her success if she truly desires to do so.

She needs healthy, consistent doses of love, support, and encouragement to succeed with nursing. Your disapproval or lack of support can make her tense, which affects her milk supply. The more relaxed she is, the faster she'll master the art of nursing. If she has problems, encourage her to consult a lactation expert, the La Leche League, or other breast-feeding support group. Discourage other people from making critical, disparaging, or disapproving remarks. Present a united front.

BOTTLE FEEDING

Advantages

- Greater mobility for mom.
- Dad can help with feedings, especially at night.
- Formula contains almost all the essential nutrients.

Disadvantages

- Formula is expensive and requires preparation.
- Formula doesn't contain immunity factors.
- Formula-fed babies have more allergies, colic, constipation, diarrhea, colds, and other contagious diseases.
- Birthweight usually doubles in 14 to 16 weeks. Overfeeding is a big problem.

However you decide to feed your baby, the most important factor is to hold and cuddle him while you do it.

FORESKIN FUTURES—CIRCUMCISION

The majority of male babies are circumcised. The decision for or against circumcision isn't related to health issues or hygiene; it's usually done for cultural and cosmetic reasons. For years, the American Academy of Pediatrics (APA) took the stance that routine circumcision was strictly cosmetic, and they didn't endorse the procedure. Insurance companies don't cover the cost of circumcision. Recently, a large study found that uncircumcised babies had a higher incidence of urinary tract infections in their first year of life, which made the APA rethink their position. Since most couples aren't influenced by health factors, anyway, it seems that the only real issue is how the procedure is done.

Painless Is Possible

Until recently, circumcisions were the only surgery done without anesthesia. Parents were consoled by the false belief that the pain sensory pathways in new babies weren't developed enough for them to really feel the pain from the procedure. Any nursery nurse could tell you that wasn't true: the howls of rage and pain echoed down the hospital halls. It took hours to console the baby, who wasn't able to sleep or eat normally due to the shock and trauma. Studies validated the physiological effects of the procedure without anesthesia.

Fortunately, many doctors now use a local anesthetic that allows the baby to be so comfortable he can literally sleep through the procedure. The anesthetized babies don't show the same disturbed behavior as those without the local. The obstetrician, not the pediatrician, does the surgery, so be sure to ask your wife's doctor if anesthesia will be used for your baby's circumcision if you choose to have

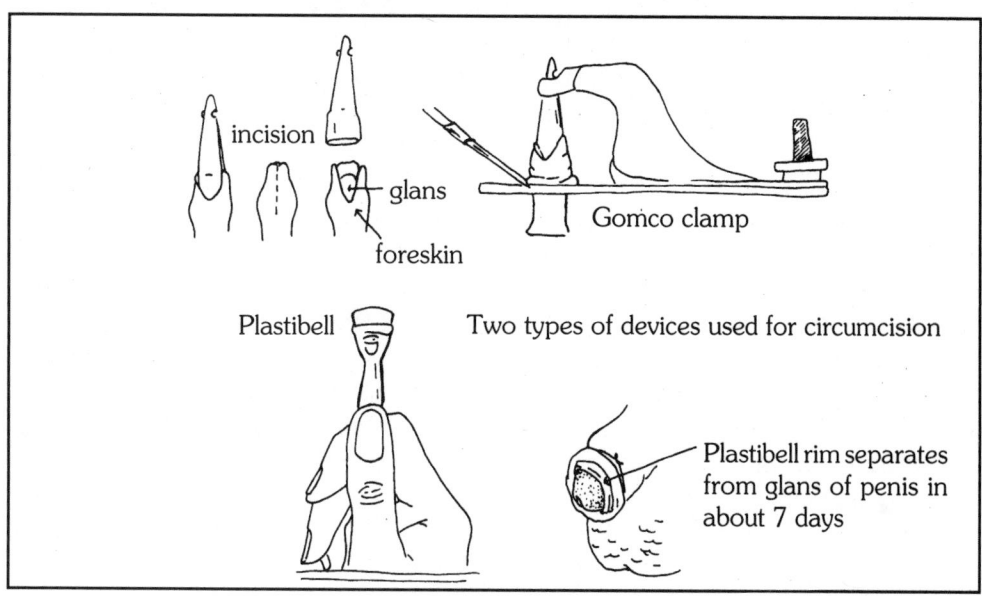

incision — glans — foreskin

Gomco clamp

Plastibell

Two types of devices used for circumcision

Plastibell rim separates from glans of penis in about 7 days

it done. If the answer is no, call the nursery of your local hospital and ask which doctors use anesthesia for circumcision. Many doctors will now do the procedure in their office, so you can have it done later. Check to see if your insurance pays for it. Hospitals and doctors usually request payment in advance.

> **"I am circumcised and we felt we would be uncomfortable trying to explain to a 5 year old why they looked different from Dad."**

BABY DOCTOR

About the seventh month of pregnancy, you want to start thinking about your baby's doctor. Here are some tips on picking one for your baby.

Interviews are very time consuming. You can streamline the process by calling and asking one of the office staff the following questions:

- What's the procedure for afterhour's coverage? Is there a call group? Do you go to the emergency room?

- How evenly is the doctor's schedule divided between illness and wellness? Are there separate hours for wellness checks so your baby won't be exposed to illness?

- Are developmental, safety, nutritional, and educational materials provided? Are staff persons qualified to provide phone advice available?

Consider how helpful and courteous the person you're speaking to is. If your questions are answered patiently and you like what you hear, make an appointment to see the doctor; it shouldn't take you more than 5 to 10 minutes to decide if your personalities and philosophies mesh. Talk to the doctor's nurse or assistant who works with her; she and the front office staff will usually be your initial contact person when you'e trying to reach the doctor. You need to decide if they'll be a help or a hindrance in getting you the information and help you need. Make your list of questions in advance to save time. You might want to know how this doctor feels about breast-feeding, if that's your choice. It's imperative that the pediatrician be supportive of your wife's efforts. How does she feel about circumcision? If you have it done, you don't want criticism for your decision.

Ideally, the doctor's practice should offer both illness and wellness care, and should provide 24 coverage. Educational material should be available. The office staff should be friendly and supportive. You're going to spend many years depending on your baby's doctor and the staff, so it's important that you trust and like each other.

BABY EQUIPMENT

The different types of equipment available for your baby is mind-boggling. Trying to sort through not only what you actually need but what 's safe for your child can seem like an overwhelming task. Whatever you decide to buy, the most important feature is safety. Injuries to children 5 years old and younger from nursery products is very high. In 1986, the U.S. Consumer Product Safety Commission reported 57,080 total injuries from products such as walkers, jumpers, cribs, cradles, strollers, carriages, and high chairs.

How do you know which products are safe? The Juvenile Products Manufacturers Association, an organization of baby equipment manufacturers, sponsors a voluntary certification program of baby products. Products are certified if they meet minimum safety performance standards developed by the American Society for Testing and Materials (ASTM). Except for child car restraints and cribs, there are no mandatory federal standards, and ASTM standards address only major hazards. For the most part, you're on your own.

To fill the much needed gap of a consumer resource, editors from *Consumer Reports Books* tested and compiled an impressive number of baby care products for consumers (see Appendix 1 Recommended Resources). This section is based largely upon their findings.

For the first 6 weeks of your baby's life, you need more of the smaller than the bigger equipment. Here's a list, starting with the smaller purchases.

What You Need
Diapers
        Cloth — 4 dozen
        Pins — 4
        Waterproof pants or wool diaper covers — 3 pair— or Disposable
        diapers, newborn size—4 case

Clothing

    T-shirts 6 month size—6 to8
    Nightgowns — 4
    Booties — 3 pair
    Small sweaters — 2
    Knitted cap (winter), brimmed hat (summer) — 1
    Zippered sacks for sleeping — 3

Bedding

    Mattress
    Bumper pad
    Waterproof pads — 4
    Fitted sheets — 4
    Lightweight blanket — 1
    Receiving blankets — 3

Toiletries

    Cotton balls
    Zinc oxide-based diaper cream
    Nasal aspirator
    Digital thermometer

Bottle-Feeding Equipment

    8 ounce plastic bottles — 4
    4 ounce plastic bottles — 4
    Extra nipples, caps, and a brush for cleaning

Breast-Feeding Equipment

    4 ounce plastic bottles for hand expressed milk — 4
    Extra nipples, caps, and brush for cleaning

Car seat restraint system
Crib

OPTIONAL
Changing table
Soft carrier

DIAPERS

Your baby will use approximately 100 diapers per week for the first 4 months of life. There are 3 ways to go on this one. Disposables are big for the convenience crowd whereas cloth diapers appeal to the more ecology minded. Diaper services offer an alternative to home laundering. Here are some facts to consider in making your choice.

Disposables are convenient, but they have their drawbacks. "Disposables" is a misnomer because these diapers aren't really disposable as far as the environment goes. In other words, they aren't biodegradable. They add considerable sewage to our already taxed landfill sites. Babies using disposables have a higher incidence of diaper rash. Disposables are also very expensive; you expect to spend around $1,000 for disposable diapers before your child is toilet trained by the age of 2 or so. Diaper service costs about half that amount. If you decide to go with the disposables, the word on the street says that Pampers Super are the best.

Cloth diapers are the most economical, and they're recyclable, and after your toddler is toilet trained, they make superb dust cloths. If you don't want to go through the hassle of home laundering, diaper service is actually a good deal if it's available in your area. The service no longer requires that their customers swish diapers in the toilet bowl; you just toss them in the bag the service provides and forget about it. Some companies provide twice-weekly service if you wish. You might want to try it and see how cloth diapers work out for you—the environment will thank you.

CLOTHING

As you can tell from the list, your baby doesn't have to be a fashion plate, at least for the first few months of life. Most babies are happy going the informal nightgown route, and buying the 6-month size ensures a longer wearing life: babies grow so fast that it's wise to think ahead. The newborn size doesn't last long enough to be practical. The zippered sacks are an especially good idea because they stay warm and you don't have to buy an expensive quilt that isn't going to be used very long.

BEDDING

A foam mattress is the least expensive and the most practical way to go. A water mattress may not fit, or it may weigh too much for the crib. A coil mattress is expensive and unnecessary. Whatever you buy must fit the crib so no gaps are between the mattress and the crib for the baby to fall into. A bumper pad helps fill any gaps between the crib and the mattress.

TOILETRIES

Cotton balls work best for keeping your baby clean those first few months. The commercial wipes have an alcohol base that can be very irritating to your baby's bottom.

Powders are totally unnecessary and may be unsafe. Babies have contracted pneumonia from inhaling powder. But if you want to use a powder, remember that cornstarch is the least expensive, and won't cause an allergic reaction. Babies already smell sweet; they don't need any help.

In the event your baby acquires irritated skin or all-out diaper rash, a zinc oxide- based cream such as Desitin will nip the problem in the bud. It provides a protective barrier and the Vitamin E fish oil base promotes healing.

A nasal aspirator is very handy for those times your baby is stuffy. It'll be a long time before he learns to blow his nose on his own. Some hospitals send one home as part of their farewell package. In any event, it's not a big ticket item.

A thermometer is a must for your medicine cabinet. If you call the doctor because you suspect your baby is ill, the first question will be about fever. The new digital thermometers are very easy to use. You can check your baby's temperature by placing the thermometer under her armpit; it isn't necessary to take a rectal temperature. If the axillary temperature is 99.8°F, call the doctor.

BOTTLES

Clear plastic bottles are the best investment because they don't break, and they're easy to clean. Expensive sterilizers or warmers are unnecessary. Bottles just need a good scrubbing with hot, soapy water or a turn in the dishwasher. If you don't mix formula in advance, you don't have to warm the bottle. Use warm tap water and you're all set to go.

CAR SEATS

Car accidents are the number one cause of death in children 1 to 4. Seventy-one percent of those deaths could have been prevented, along with 67 percent of the injuries incurred if an approved car seat restraint system had been used. States now have child safety laws that mandate the use of such a system. Your baby's first ride home should be in a federally approved, rear-facing car seat.

One type of car seat such as the Century 570 Infant Car Seat and Cosco TLC Infant Car Seat, is designed for the newborn to 20-pound size. These seats can also double as a portable infant seat for activities such as napping and relaxing outside the crib.

The most practical restraint system is the five point harness. This device can be used from birth to 40 pounds. You can use it in the recommended rear-facing arrangement until your toddler is ready to face the other way. The five point harness is considered the safest of all the restraint systems. Two recommended models are the Century 1000 and the Kolcraft Ultra Ride.

Before purchasing a restraint system, be sure it fits the back seat of your car; try it out before you buy it. Read the directions carefully and follow them to the letter. Failure to adjust the device properly invalidates the principle for which you bought it: the safety of your baby.

CRIB

The crib is an important purchase from both the monetary and safety aspects. A safe crib is one that has side rails or slats no farther than 2 -3/8 inches apart. The mattress should be adjustable so that it can be lowered as your baby grows and learns to sit and stand up. There should be no spaces between the mattress and the sides and ends of the crib. When shopping for a crib, look for one with a smooth finish. Run your hand over all the parts your baby would touch. Check it carefully for decorations that might become loose and present a hazard to your baby when he gets to the exploration stage. Try the side rail to see if it goes up and down smoothly.

If you don't consider yourself very handy at putting things together, ask the store to deliver it assembled. Before your baby arrives, go over the crib carefully and check for loose screws and bolts and anything else that might fall off.

OPTIONAL ITEMS
Changing Table

A changing table isn't necessary, but it's nice to have. A safe table is sturdy and won't collapse. The wooden nursery chests with a fold-down wooden adapter are the least safe; the chest has been known to topple over if the baby is placed on the outside edge. The fold-up table with baskets underneath to hold diapers and other equipment are the most practical and take up less space. Whatever table you choose, never take your hand off your baby while he's on the table.

Soft Carrier

Soft carriers such as the Snugli can be used from birth to about 4 months of age. They offer the advantage of freeing your arms for other things while cuddling your baby. Most babies love the close contact and find it very comforting. The soft carriers are particularly appreciated when you have a fussy baby.

If you purchase a soft carrier, consider which time of the year you'll be using it. For instance, you don't want a heavy corduroy for summer use.

A FINAL WORD

Be a discriminating shopper, particularly if money is a problem; invest in a copy of the *Guide to Baby Products* book listed in Appendix 1. The authors give a number of very practical alternatives to expensive items such as cribs and changing tables. There's a lot of equipment you really don't need, and many items can be unsafe. Do your homework before buying yourself into finnacial oblivion— it's not hard to do.

ΔΔΔ

$\boxed{6}$

DOCTOR DATA

THREE'S COMPANY

Because of the intense nature of the experience, a woman usually develops a close relationship with her doctor, whether the physician is male or female. This is only natural since her doctor shares every aspect of her pregnancy from the beginning to the end. You have to deal with the fact that your wife has another significant other in her life besides you for now. Many men have uncomfortable feelings about their wife having such an intimate relationship with her doctor, even though it's strictly professional. You have two options: you can decide to ignore the whole thing and keep your distance, or you can become a part of that pregnancy relationship.

Many men never darken the door of their wife's obstetrician. Some may go just once; others try to make every office visit they can. It serves your best interests to meet her doctor at least once before labor and delivery. If problems develop during the pregnancy, you'll feel more secure and comfortable having met her caregiver. When the big day finally arrives and you head for the hospital, you'll be grateful for any and all familiar, friendly faces—especially her doctor's.

When you accompany her on your first visit to meet her doctor, you'll experience, first hand, how the queen's husband must feel as you follow behind her. You may feel like a fifth wheel as she basks in the glow of attention and affection the staff bestows on her. Nowdays, they're used to including dad into the happy group, so relax and let them bond to you; they're always impressed with husbands who take an interest.

> **"What I look for in a doctor is honest answers, and one who doesn't mind being questioned."**

During your visit is a good time to obtain answers to any questions or concerns you may have. Her doctor will be happy to discuss them with you. Remember, this is a get-acquainted, fact- finding mission, not an excursion into enemy-occupied territory. Be friendly and relaxed. Although it's always high on the concern list of many couples, it's counterproductive and usually futile to ask for her doctor's personal cesarean birth rate. Most doctors don't keep track, and there's currently no way you can check the validity of the statistics even if they're given to you. Hospitals have that information but are unlikely to share it with you. In reality, cesarean birth statistics don't always give valid insight into the quality of obstetrics being practiced because too many variables enter into making the decision to do a cesarean. Refer to Chapter 12 "Special Delivery" for more insight.

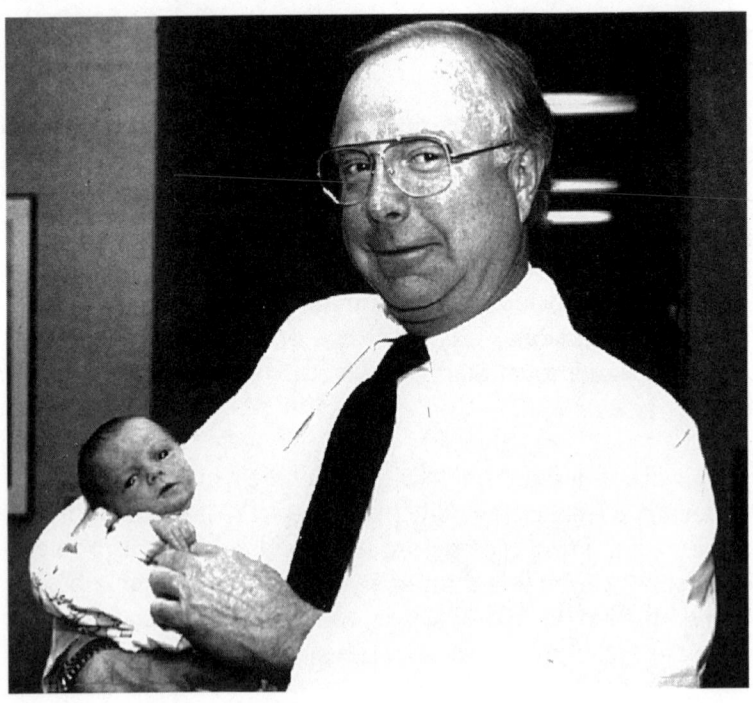

> **"The qualities most important to me in a doctor are open communication, thoroughness, good bedside manner, and humor."**
>
> **"The doctor should be a great listener and consider all inputs by both of us. He should be sensitive to our requests and open minded....and be current with the latest theories and practices."**

If this is a first visit with the doctor for both you and your wife, here are some sample questions you and your wife might ask:

Questions for the Doctor

- In which hospital do you primarily practice? What do you like best about that hospital?
- What is your policy regarding ultrasound exams during pregnancy? How many do you routinely do? If you do an ultrasound, can the husband and children be present?
- If I develop a complication, will you still care for me, or transfer my care elsewhere? If yes, where would I go?
- What birth options are you comfortable providing?
- What procedures do you routinely require during labor?
- What is your policy regarding preps, enemas, fetal monitoring, and IVs?
- How do you feel about support persons? Do you have a limit as to numbers?
- What is your approach to episiotomy and positions during delivery?
- What are your preferences regarding medications and anesthesia for labor and delivery?
- How do you feel about vaginal birth after cesarean? Do you offer that option?
- How many doctors are in your call group? What are their names? Do the doctors in your call group share you birthing philosophy? How do they differ?
- Does the office provide prepared childbirth or other educational classes? What kind?

IMPORTANT INFORMATION

Some of your questions may relate to insurance coverage. If you have insurance with maternity benefits, your first step is to know exactly what is and is not covered. If you haven't checked with your insurance carrier, the office manager or billing clerk would be able to help you clarify any questions you have. Here are some samples:

- What is the fee for a vaginal birth? Cesarean birth?
- What is the preferred method of payment (full in advance, payment not due until delivery, or negotiated arrangement)?
- What insurance plans do you accept?
- Which hospitals in my area accept my insurance?
- What is the total reimbursement for the doctor?
- What is the total reimbursement allowance for hospital costs?
- How many hospital days are allowed for a vaginal birth and cesarean birth?
- What type of hospital room does my plan provide for? Private? Semiprivate or Ward?
- How is payment handled for services? Direct payment to physician? Reimbursement to me after delivery?
- What obstetrical costs are covered?
  Ultrasound?
  Blood tests?
  Amniocentesis?
  Fetal well-being tests (stress and nonstress testing)?
  Medications?
- Is there coverage for neonatal or pediatric care?
- What coverage is there should complications occur?

ROUTINE TESTS

A number of tests are done for your wife to rule out and assess any potential problems during pregnancy. Following is an overview of the routine tests and procedures usually done at her prenatal workup and other tests that may be done when needed.

Blood Count (Hemoglobin and Hematocrit)

This test detects anemia. It is repeated around 28 weeks to monitor if blood volume has expanded adequately. A woman's hematocrit normally decreases during the second trimester because of increased plasma volume and the slower increase in red cell production. Since the decrease is a healthy sign, some practitioners argue against routinely giving iron supplements, but most do.

Urinalysis and Culture

Since symptoms may not be present, screening for infection and other kidney disease is important. "Silent" infections can cause preterm labor symptoms.

Blood Type and Rh Factor

This test establishes if there's a potential risk to the baby because of incompatibility between you and your wife's blood types. See the Rh Incompatibility section in Chapter 10, "Potential Problems."

Antibody Screen

This blood test detects antibodies in your wife's blood that may be potentially harmful to the baby.

Rubella (Measles) Antibody Titer

This test determines immunity to measles. Nonimmune rates in women are around 10 percent. Measles produce serious congenital deformities if the mother is infected during pregnancy. Immunization for nonimmune women is done *after* delivery.

Serology (VDRL)

Positive rates for syphllis are very low, but testing is required by state law.

Blood Sugar

This test screens for potential gestational diabetes (pregnancy induced glucose intolerance). Pregnant women are more prone to this condition since the hormones of pregnancy inhibit insulin production. A high carbohydrate meal or 50-gram glucose drink is taken and the blood sugar level tested in 1 or 2 hours. Experts recommend all pregnant women be screened during pregnancy. See the Diabetes section in Chapter 10.

OTHER TESTS
Chlamydia

Chlamydia is a common sexually transmitted disease, with 3 million new infections annually in the United States. There are no known adverse effects on pregnancy, but the newborn baby whose mother has the chlamydia virus in her cervix can contract eye infections or pneumonitis after birth. Chlamydia, detected during pregnancy, can be treated effectively before delivery to eliminate the risk to the baby and mother.

Chicken Pox

Five percent of adults escape contracting chicken pox as a child. Fortunately, even with no history of having the virus, only one-fourth of adults are susceptible. A lab test detects immunity if your wife is uncertain whether she's had it. Chicken pox can be very serious in pregnancy. If your wife isn't immune and is exposed to the virus, she can be treated with zoster immune globulin (ZIG) while pregnant. Have her talk to her doctor. If she is immune, she doesn't have to worry about being exposed.

Cytomegalovirus (CMV) and Parvovirus

CMV exposure may occur in health care workers, school teachers, and day care providers. Parvovirus causes "Fifth disease," a fairly common viral illness in school children. If the mother contracts the infection during pregnancy, the risk to the baby is very small. If she's exposed to either virus, she can call her doctor for further advice.

Human Immunodeficiency Virus (HIV)

HIV is a sexually transmitted disease that causes AIDS (acquired immunodeficiency syndrome). The virus attacks the body's immune system, resulting in a loss of resistance to various infections. The virus may be present in the blood many years before symptoms of

AIDS develop. Ninety percent of AIDS cases have occurred in homosexual or bisexual men, intravenous drug users, and those who have received HIV-contaminated blood or blood products. In cities with a high rate of IV drug users, HIV in pregnant women is becoming more prevalent.

Obstetricians are concerned about HIV because the pregnant woman can unknowingly transmit the virus to her unborn child. Any pregnant woman who has had sexual contact at some time with someone in the high-risk groups for carrying the AIDS virus needs to discuss it with her physician.

Hepatitis B (serum hepatitis)

It is possible to carry the hepatitis B virus and not have symptoms. The virus can be transmitted to the pregnant woman's baby during delivery. When a pregnant woman is identified as a virus carrier, treatment can be given to the baby at the delivery to prevent infection.

Health care workers and Southeast Asians are considered at higher risk for being carriers of the virus. In some areas, hepatitis B testing is routine for all pregnant women. If your wife is in the high-risk category, have her talk to her doctor.

Toxoplasmosis

If you're a cat owner or your wife works in the veterinary field, this one is for you. Toxoplasmosis is an infection resulting from contact with airborne protozoa from cat feces or from eating contaminated raw or rare meat. The infection isn't serious unless it's the first occurrence for the pregnant women. If your wife is in the at-risk category, her doctor can test her to see if she has had a previous infection. It's nice to have reassurance that there's no risk to your baby. Ideally, she should be tested *before* she becomes pregnant. During pregnancy, you'll have to be the one to empty the kitty litter. Sorry.

APPOINTMENTS

Office visits are monthly until 32 weeks, every 2 weeks until 36 weeks, and usually weekly during the last month. Visits may be fairly brief but very important. Besides answering questions, the doctor will evaluate and record several things, including:

1. **Blood pressure** (BP). Normally your wife's BP decreases by the second trimester. If her BP increases during the second trimester, it may be one of the signs of preeclampsia, a dangerous disease for both her and the baby.

2. **Weight.** A steady pattern of weight gain is important to your baby's growth. Unusual weight gain, more than 2 pounds in 1 week, may be the first sign of preeclampsia. Failure to gain weight may signal growth problems for the baby.

3. **Uterine size.** The uterus is measured to detect if the baby is growing appropriately for his gestational age. A larger than normal size could be twins or indicate maternal diabetes. A smaller than normal size might indicate a baby with intrauterine growth retardation (IUGR). See Chapter 10.

4. **Fetal Heart Rate.** The baby's heart rate is listened to at each visit; it doesn't provide reliable information regarding the baby's well-being, but it's reassuring for the mom to hear it. There's no validity to predicting sex according to heart rate. It tends to be faster in early pregnancy and slows as the central nervous system matures. Usual heart rates are between 120 to160 beats per minute.

5. **Fetal Movement.** An active baby is usually a healthy baby. It's a good idea if your wife becomes acquainted with your baby's wake and sleep cycles (activity patterns). If she detects a noticeable decrease in the baby's *usual* activity, she should call and check with her doctor.

6. **Urine Testing.** A urine sample is traditionally tested every visit for protein and sugar. Many normal pregnant women spill sugar in their urine. A blood sugar test is the preferred way to screen for diabetes. Protein is checked to detect preeclampsia, but weight gain and BP are earlier indicators of the presence of the disease. Refer to the Preeclampsia section in Chapter 10.

As you can see, a lot of thought and effort go into helping you have an uneventful pregnancy and a healthy baby.

ΔΔΔ

7

PREPARED CHILDBIRTH

THE DARK AGES

The attitudes surrounding childbirth have gone through some interesting changes in the last several decades. In the "Fabulous Fifties," the details of birthing babies was left entirely up to the doctor. It was considered very serious business, much too complicated to worry the womenfolk and too gruesome for the men.

At that time, the "wake me when it's over" approach was pretty standard. Mom was drugged into a stupor so she wouldn't remember much of the whole event. Everyone figured that if she could recall what happened, she wouldn't ever be willing to go through it again. She'd be tempted to adopt a new form of birth control by lighting a gasoline-filled trench surrounding her bed. Not a happy thought.

Dad was relegated to the sidelines and mostly forgotten. His only contribution to this life-changing event was to be nervous and pace the waiting room, where he could chew his nails in anxious anticipation. No self-respecting male would have entertained the unlikely thought of seeing his baby being born. Only "preverts" had subversive ideas like that. The FBI put those people on their special deranged list as threats to the national security. It was the best of times; it was the worst of times.

By the late 60s and into the 70s, a major revolution in childbirth approaches swept the country. Dr. Lamaze from France advocated "natural" childbirth as the alternative to our "unnatural" methods. He sought to educate and eliminate fear associated with the childbirth process and give control back to the mother. Dr. Bradley from this country added his brand of childbirth options and gave us the Bradley Method. Even though the two approaches varied somewhat in theory and practice, the followers of both methods were convinced everyone should have "cold turkey" as the entrée on their childbirth menu. We all had to be awake, pay attention, be quiet, and *breathe* properly. These practices mated well with the Aquarian philosophy of peace, love, and togetherness. In this organic era of natural everything, we now had "natural" childbirth. It was a match made in heaven for a while.

Expectant couples began attending classes to receive their indoctrination in the ground rules. **Do** pant, breathe, and concentrate. No drugs for pain. No screaming aloud allowed. The uninhibited "vocalizing" heard in the previous decade was no longer acceptable. As time went on, the labor bed became the feminine equivalent of the battlefield where warrior status was bestowed. Female macho was in vogue. The only acceptable pain relief was an old silver bullet clenched tightly between the teeth Lone Ranger style. If you gave into the pain, you had failed.

Dad's role was to make sure his mate lived up to everyone's expectations. Wipe her sweaty brow, keep the ice chips coming, and fend off anyone who might interfere with the "natural" process at work. Giving into pain wasn't acceptable. No one wanted to go back to the childbirth class reunion and admit they failed. A drug- free labor was a badge of honor. Many were called, but few were chosen.

Fortunately over time, the rigid rules began to bend. After all, the "me" generation believed in doing their own thing, and suffering wasn't high on their list. Attitudes and practices became more flexible. Fern rooms flourished as hospitals across the country offered "homestyle" rooms for labor and delivery. Devotees of Dr. Bradley and Dr. Lamaze began concentrating more on the commonalties than the differences in the two childbirth techniques. Instructors started mixing and matching techniques and even dared to suggest that a little medication might be all right after all. A few brave souls even dared to declare all that fancy breathing didn't produce a painless labor as advertised by the more radical factions in childbirth education. A live and let live attitude flowered, much to everyone's relief. "Natural" childbirth gave way to "Prepared" childbirth in this more enlightened era.

During the 80s, dad found himself promoted from water boy to head coach. In the 90s, expectations for this expanded role are many. You are expected to train intensively with your mate, attend classes, identify the various phases of labor, and have all the appropriate interventions burned in your brain. You must be familiar with the routine equipment for the training bag, including lollipops, pillows, focusing objects, cold washcloth, and know the basics of the fetal monitor. You have to be alert and flexible, and cheer her on in her darkest hour at 8 centimeters. You are expected to be sensitive, warm, and comforting, even when she has momentarily lost her sanity and begins using language that would deliver shivers to even a salty old sea dog. It's a tough job, and the mission can be yours should you choose to accept.

Even if your wife plans to have an epidural for labor and delivery, **childbirth classes are still a very important part of pregnancy.** Classes can relieve both your anxiety by giving information on labor physiology and the range of birthing options offered in your community. You then have the knowledge to make informed decisions that best suit your style and personalities.

Classes also provide the opportunity to share your pregnancy/birthing experience with other couples. A supportive group is a most welcome addition to this happy time in your life.

The basic theory behind prepared childbirth, whether it be Lamaze, Bradley, Fitzhugh, or Dick-Reid, is predicated upon the same principles:

BASIC THEORY OF PREPARED CHILDBIRTH

Self-awareness
Self-control through programmed exercises
Reduction of pain through education and knowledge of the labor and delivery process

Remember that the key word here is *reduction*. Many couples still falsely expect their childbirth exercises to completely eliminate pain. Nothing but a good epidural will do that. The exercises you and your wife practice during her pregnancy are meant to develop her powers of concentration so she can alter her pain perception and maintain self-control during the labor and delivery process.

LEARNING TO RELAX

FIRST LEVEL

1. Take three slow, deep breaths. At the height of the inhalation breath, pause for about 2 seconds before releasing the air. Breathe naturally and rhythmically in through your nose and out your mouth, with lips slightly pursed. Imagine a balloon inflating and deflating in your belly.

2. Close your eyes tightly and frown. Relax the tensed muscles.
3. Grit your teeth and then relax, letting your tongue drop from the roof of your mouth.

4. Bend your neck forward, and then drop your chin on your chest.

5. Raise your shoulders at attention, and then let them droop forward into a comfortable slump.

6. Clench your right hand as if squeezing a ball, and then relax. Repeat with left hand.

7. Take a very deep breath. Fill your lungs and hold your breath for 2 to 3 seconds, and then exhale fully.

8. Pull in your stomach muscles as tightly as possible and let go.
9. Squeeze the muscles in your buttocks and perineum (Kegel's exercise), and then relax.

10. Tense the muscles in your right leg, and then relax. Repeat with your left leg.

11. Flex your right foot. Point your toes toward your body and then relax. Repeat with left foot.

12. Feel the feeling of having your whole body relaxed.

SECOND LEVEL

1. Breathe slowly and rhythmically.
2. Tense face muscles and then relax.
3. Tense neck and shoulders and then relax.
4. Clench hand and tense arms, and then relax.
5. Tense abdomen and buttocks, then relax.
6. Tense legs and feet, and then relax.

THIRD LEVEL

1. Use rhythmic breathing.
2. Relax your face.
3. Relax upper body.
4. Relax lower body.

Relaxation exercises

Review the commonly used exercises on the opposite page. You'll both learn them in class so you can get a head start if you wish.

Use visualization to aid in relaxing. See relaxation as a white light of energy flowing in through the top of your head. As the white light advances downward, see the tension being pushed out of your body through your finger tips and toes until it disappears.

The only difference in the three levels of relaxation is practice. As your wife becomes more aware of her body and learns to relax, she can hasten the process to reach the relaxed state. You're working to attain a conditioned response that will distract her from the pain during contractions. Concentrating on a focal point provides distraction during contractions to alter her perception of pain. The focal point can be external if she prefers to keep her eyes open. Place an object or picture at her eye level to keep her in a comfortable position. If she prefers to keep her eyes closed, she can focus her mind's eye on a favorite relaxing vision, such as a place, like a mountain or a still lake. Or she could be in a forest or standing under a waterfall with warm water cascading over her, relaxing her whole body. Memorize her favorite place so you can describe it to her during labor. For example, with the waterfall you can say to her "You're standing under your waterfall; warm water is cascading over your entire body. Feel it washing away the pain as it moves slowly and peacefully down your body." Use a very soft, quiet, hypnotic voice that will elicit that conditioned response over time and with practice.

BREATHING EXERCISES

Concentrating on rhythmic breathing can help your wife relax. Everyone has a comfortable breathing pace; attuning to her own breathing rhythms helps her avoid hyperventilating. Anxiety precedes hyperventilation, not the reverse. With hyperventilation, fingers and face feel numb and tingly, and there's a shortness of breath. It's very uncomfortable and distracting, especially during labor. Rebreathing air in a paper bag doesn't reverse the results of hyperventilating. The best intervention is to reverse the anxiety attack, allowing her to slow her breathing.

Childbirth instructors teach three types of breathing techniques. There are no specific times to use each technique during labor. It's best not to start using the breathing exercises until the contractions definitely demand attention as they become regular and intense. If the exercises are started too early in labor, she'll wear herself out. Try them at various stages to see which one of the three works best for her at the time. She can switch back and forth, but return to exercise1 as quickly as possible. Some women prefer to use a deep inhalation and full exhalation (cleansing breath) to signal the beginning and end of contractions.

Exercise 1 —Slow Paced Breathing

This exercise is very relaxing and helps avoid hyperventilation. Slow-paced breathing is the type uses during the relaxation exercises. The rate is usually half of the normal breathing pace. Both chest and abdominal muscles are used with this technique. It's less tiring than the others and enhances a calm, relaxed state.

Exercise 2—Modified-Paced Breathing

Breathe no faster than twice the normal rate. This one can be used when the contractions become more intense. Be careful she doesn't start hyperventilating. When the contraction is over, quickly return to exercise1.

Exercise 3—Patterned Breathing (pant-blow)

Pant blow breathing has the same rate as exercise 2 but combines a pattern of inhaling and slow blow exhaling. Remind your wife to exhale as if she is softly blowing out a candle: short bursts of breath with a very shallow intake of air. The blowing technique can be useful to avoid pushing. If she takes a deep breath, she'll have an uncontrollable urge to push. By concentrating on exhale-blowing, she can refrain from taking that deep breath that makes her want to push.

ADVANCE ADVICE

Your participation in prepared childbirth classes will help your wife keep her options open for labor and delivery. She'll need your help in making decisions during labor. She needs to be realistic about her pain threshold. If she becomes hysterical over a hangnail, consider the epidural option. If she can smile on a bed of nails, the childbirth exercises or silver bullet may be enough. Use the exercises you learn in class to meet her needs and be flexible. Don't let her set herself up for a guilt trip because she needed some pain medication or had an epidural. She'll really need your patience and support. It's nice to know how you can help your wife and give your new baby a loving welcome into the world.

ΔΔΔ

BIRTH OPTIONS

Hospitals want your business, so they're more willing than ever to provide you with the services you want and forgo what you'd rather not have as long as it doesn't compromise safety. For example, most doctor's have discarded routine shaves and enemas. Continuous fetal monitoring and IVs are used only for complications during labor. If your wife is considered low-risk, she may be monitored but the monitoring is limited to an initial 20-minute baseline strip on admission and repeated only for 10 minutes every hour or so. The majority of hospitals welcome dad into the labor and delivery rooms. Many hospitals welcome as many support people as you want. A number of birth options are possible.

FAMILY CENTERED CARE (FCC)

With FCC, the entire family's needs are considered from admission to discharge. If desired, the whole family, including extended family, remain together during the hospital stay. If a cesarean birth is necessary, the father and a support person can both attend the birth. There are very liberal guidelines for visitation and the numbers of family and extended family permitted. Sibling are welcome. Your baby stays with you as much as you like.

FCC is a welcome addition to any obstetrical unit. Everyone benefits. The term FCC is generic, but the execution of the concept isn't. If your prospective hospital doesn't provide the preceding guidelines, it also doesn't provide FCC. Check it out.

SHORT STAY PROGRAMS

Ten years ago, the average hospital stay for a new mom was 3 days, but now it's 24 hours. Some hospitals offer an even shorter stay of 12 hours or less. Check your insurance program to see what they allow so you can plan in advance.

With the short stay program, your wife loses out on the teaching support from the nurses, but she'll get more rest at home, *if she has help*. Once home, you can both get better acquainted with the baby and establish a routine sooner. There are other resources to help the first-time parents who need encouragement and advice. A good baby book is an invaluable resource, as is the nurse in the pediatrician's office. For the breast-feeding mother, the La Leche League and the International Childbirth Education Association (ICEA) provides support. Check to see if the hospital provides follow-up care at home.

SINGLE-ROOM MATERNITY CARE

Single-room maternity care is the new wave of obstetrics. One room serves as a labor, delivery, recovery, and postpartum room. Even though many older hospitals can't offer total maternity care in one room because of building constraints, they do the best they can. Most hospitals have mom labor and deliver in one room and then move her to the maternity floor for recovery and postpartum. It's still a great improvement. It's truly a relief to most women not to have to keep moving from room to room for each phase of birth. There's nothing worse than trying not to push while moving onto or off a gurney. With single-room maternity care, mom can keep her baby in the room as long as she likes or send her back to the nursery for a while.

FREESTANDING BIRTH CENTERS (FSBCs)

FSBCs are usually staffed by certified nurse midwives (CNMs) with obstetrician backup. They're operated independently of a hospital. Only low-risk women who remain low-risk in labor are allowed to deliver in the FSBC. Technology such as fetal monitoring is rarely used. Laboring women are encouraged to stay out of bed and use a variety of positions to alleviate pain and speed progress.

Around 13 percent of women who labor in FSBCs require transfer to a hospital because of complications. Outcomes for babies delivered in an FSBC and the hospital setting are the same. FSBCs are not widely available, so you'll have to look around.

ANESTHESIA

Of late, a new sentiment is creeping across the country. "No pain, no gain" is now passé. The winds of change are whispering a new mantra in our ears: "Be awake, be alert, and don't hurt."

Epidural anesthesia is experiencing a resurgence in popularity, and many hospitals now offer this option. With epidural anesthesia, mom is numb from the waist down (see the Anesthesia and Pain Relief section in Chapter 13, "Labor and Birth").

The epidural is most often administered somewhere during the mid-part of the active phase of labor, giving mom a chance to use the breathing techniques she learned in childbirth class and allowing you an opportunity to star in your role as coach. The rest of labor is pain free, and other types of pain medications aren't needed. It's a great option for women not interested in experiencing labor pains from start to finish.

If you want to explore this option, start talking to her doctor now. Some hospitals may offer epidurals during the day but not after hours. They can also be expensive, and few, if any, insurance plans cover the cost for use with a vaginal birth.

IN OR OUT?

Dad's presence during the birth process has become almost mandatory, which doesn't leave much flexibility for those of you who don't feel you could cope with such an intense situation. It has nothing to do with how much you love your wife or the baby. If you're particularly dreading the thought of seeing the actual birth, discuss your fears with your wife and her doctor. Prepare your wife, and give yourself the option to bow out of the actual delivery if you feel the need. Step outside at the last minute and come back when the baby is born. Some men just close their eyes or stay at the head of the bed with their wife so they can't really see anything. Chances are, even if you think you don't want to be present, you might find your fears have vanished when the time actually arrives. Keep your options open.

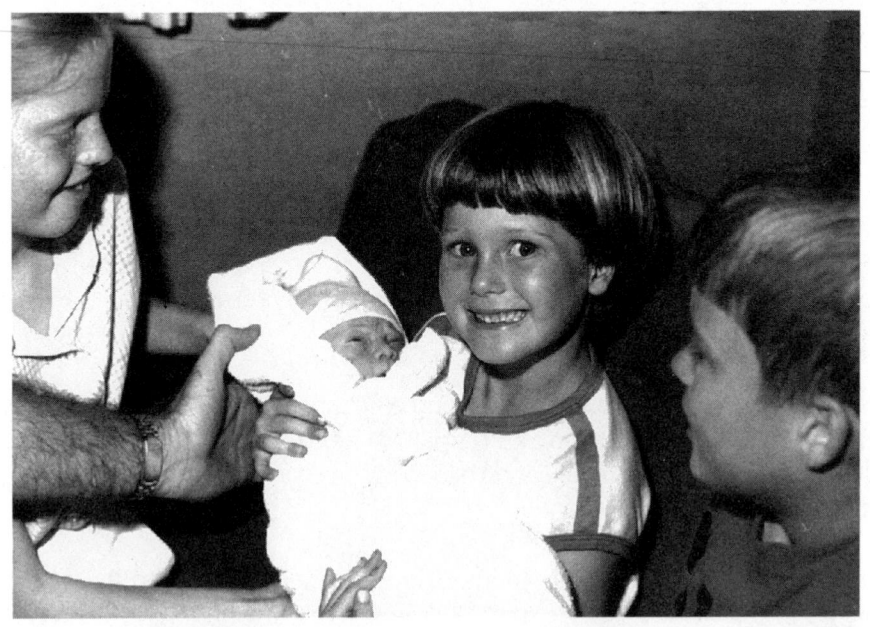

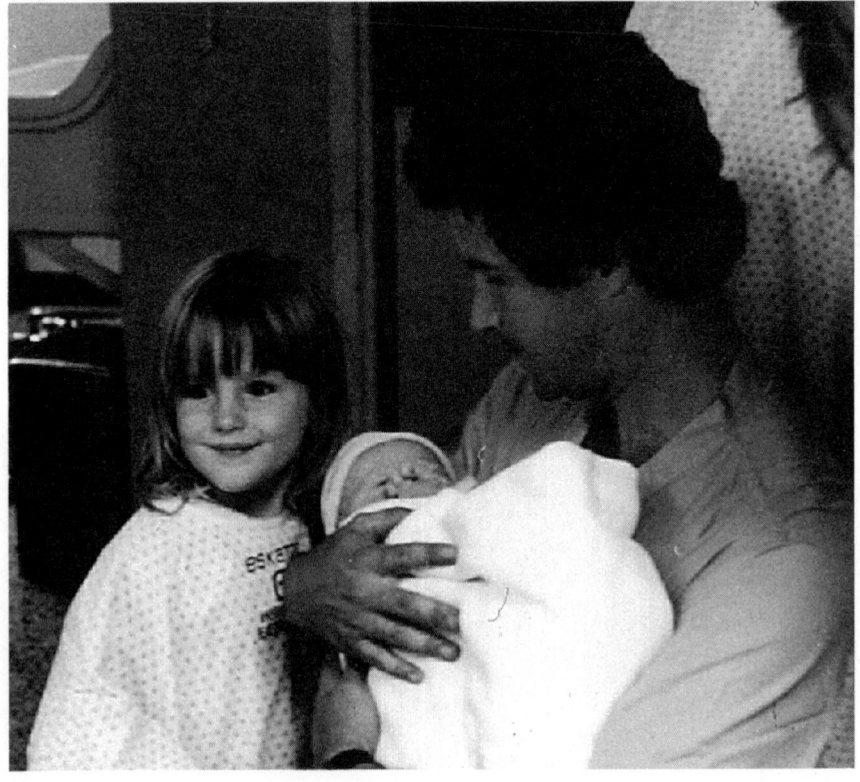

SIBLING PARTICIPATION

It's still too early to tell if there's any detrimental or lasting effects on the psyches of those kids who attend the birth process. The detractors predict that little boys will grow up impotent and little girls will head for the nearest convent at puberty. You have to decide what suits your family. Having your kids participate in the birth experience requires common sense and some preparation.

Discuss the possibility with your children. How do they feel about being there? How does your wife feel about them seeing her au naturel? Try to evaluate if they can handle the process of seeing their mother in pain.

If everyone wants to be there, they need to know where babies come from, how they get here, and a preview of the panting, blowing, and funny faces their mother will be making during labor. Check the Recommended Resources for a book to help in that preparation.

If you decide to have your children with you during labor and birth, provide a designated support person just for them. Some children find the experience too stimulating; others find it boring. Give each child something to do, such as taking pictures, getting ice chips, or rubbing mom's feet to relax her. Some women prefer to have the kids leave at the moment of birth and then have them rejoin her right afterward to hold the baby.

More hospitals are willing to let siblings be present for the birth of their new baby brother or sister. Some hospitals even have orientation classes for kids to help acclimate them to the hospital setting.

HOME OR HOSPITAL?

The decision to give birth out of a hospital setting is usually an emotional one for most couples. Some couples want their birth experience to be strictly a family affair with dad assisting the birth of the baby. A previous negative birth experience in the hospital may deepen the desire for a home birth.

Only 1 percent of couples stay home to have their babies. Most deliveries (90 percent) go smoothly, but 2 percent involve serious, unanticipated threats to mother and baby. You have to decide how much you're willing to risk. California reported a stillbirth rate that was twice as high for home births as hospital births. Hospitals offer greater safety because of the availability of trained personnel and equipment.

If you're considering a home birth strictly because you want to deliver your own baby, consider asking your wife's doctor if you can participate in the delivery. Some doctors are very flexible and will let you join in, or at least cut the umbilical cord. It never hurts to ask, especially if it means a lot to you and you don't really have anything against delivering in the hospital.

If you and your wife are in the 1 percent category, you have a lot of homework to do.

If your state has licensed midwives, you're in luck. If not, here are some important factors for you to consider:

- For safety's sake, you need to be reasonably assured your wife has a pelvis that is adequate in size. She also needs to be evaluated by an obstetrician for other risk factors. Complications such as twins, diabetes, preeclampsia, or a history of preterm labor are absolutely unsuitable for a home birth.

- Interview your prospective midwife carefully. Ask her how many babies has she delivered (50 is an appropriate number). What training has she had? Has she had any experience in resuscitating a baby? Does she have an emergency plan for prolapsed cord, bleeding, or a breech delivery? Is she willing to care for your wife if she develops preeclampsia or other complications? If she will, find someone else—she doesn't know her limitations.

BETTER SHOP AROUND

Once you have decided which birthing options you want, call the hospitals in your area where your wife's doctor practices and investigate the services they have to offer. Here are some sample questions:

QUESTIONS FOR THE HOSPITAL

- What types of birthing rooms do you offer? Traditional? Single-room, labor/delivery/recovery/postpartum (LDRP), or a combination?

- Who do you allow for support persons? How many? Do you let children attend births? If you do, does the hospital offer preparation classes?

- Do you allow video cameras during delivery?

- If a cesarean has to be done, do you allow support persons in the operating room?

- Do you offer vaginal birth after cesarean?

- What types of anesthesia for delivery do you provide? Is epidural anesthesia available?

- Do you have 24-hour anesthesia coverage in the hospital, or do you use on-call people after hours?

- After delivery, how soon can our baby begin breast-feeding?

- Does the baby have to stay in the nursery, or can we have unlimited access to him?

- How soon after delivery do you usually discharge patients?

You can add or delete questions to the list depending on what's important to you. Don't ask nurses about hospital fees; they don't usually know about those things. Call a few childbirth educators and get their input. There are many resources of information out there. Take advantage of the tours the hospitals provide. Get a first- hand glimpse of their labor rooms, nursery, and maternity floor before you make a decision. Good hunting!

ΔΔΔ

9

PREPARED PARENTING

Expectant couples commonly take prepared childbirth classes, but who do you know who goes to parenting classes to get ready for the awesome responsibility of raising a child? It seems illogical that we need a license to drive and get married, but nothing is required to be a parent. Most of us have poor training for the important task of nurturing and guiding a child to grow into a healthy, happy, well- adjusted adult. It's a responsibility that can weigh very heavily on expectant parents.

TIMELY TRENDS

Being a dad used to be fairly simple. A good father was one who was responsible and a good provider—period. He wasn't expected to venture into the female-dominated territory of diaper changing and other related child care duties, let alone share feelings, be vulnerable, and communicate caringly so as not to damage the delicate psyches of the children. Times have definitely changed, but how much?

New research in the 70s and 80s began to look at the evolving role of the father in the family and ways to help men be the kind of fathers they most wanted to be.

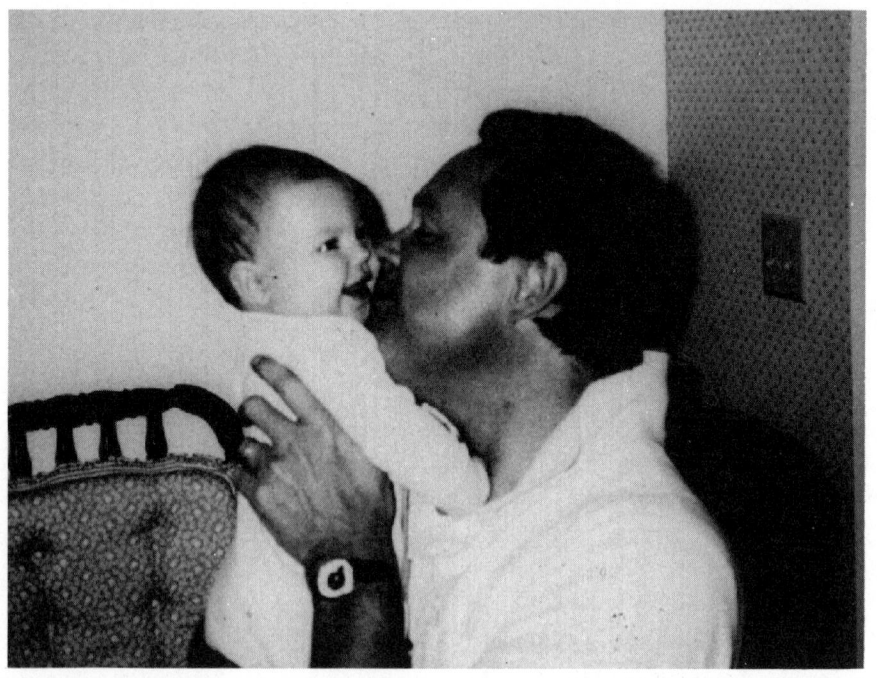

Dr. Ronald Levant, director of the Fatherhood Project conducted at Boston University from 1983 to 1988, found that men really wanted to change the approach and terms of the father-child relationship. These dads wanted to have a warm, open, intimate, and even tender relationship with their children instead of the traditional respectful but distant one most of them had experienced with their own fathers. With training programs, the Fatherhood Project helped fathers improve their communication and relationship skills with their children.

"My greatest concern centers on providing monetary and emotional support.

James Levine, director of the Fatherhood Project at the Families and Work Institute (FWI) in New York City, has conducted research since 1981 on the family/work dilemmas most men face. FWI provided the following statistics from various sources, such as Gallup polls and *Fortune* and *Gentlemen's Quarterly* magazines, all showing that fatherhood has a high priority for most men. More men are involved right from the beginning. The percentage of men present in the delivery room has increased over the years—16 percent in 1961, 27 percent 1971, and 80 percent in 1984.

"As far as taking care of the baby, it will be a 50/50 deal with us."

"I want to do as much as possible."

FWI Statistics

- 73 percent of men feel their family is the most important facet of their life.
- 54 percent feel that for a man to be a father is the most satisfying accomplishment.
- 87 percent feel that a father's role is just as important as a mother's in raising children.
- 73 percent of men take time away from work specifically to attend to their children.
- 30 percent refused a job, promotion, or transfer because it would have meant less family time.
- 81 percent of dads take a bigger part in child care duties than their fathers did.
- 62 percent spend more time with their children than their fathers did.
- 55 percent share equally in child care responsibility.

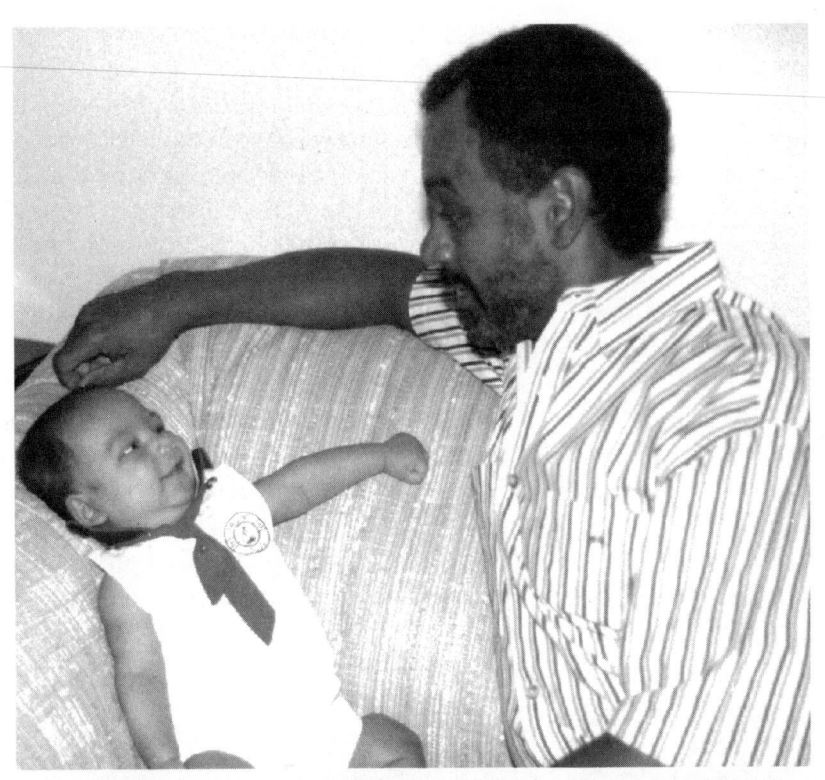

DYSFUNCTIONAL DILEMMAS

Experts in marriage and family counseling, such as John Bradshaw, offer the theory that most if not all families are dysfunctional to some degree. In the dysfunctional family, communication is either destructive or nonexistent. Emotions are repressed, denied, and not shared. In this atmosphere, nurturing isn't possible, and the needs of the individual family members are unmet. In this atmosphere, children aren't able to complete certain emotional developmental tasks that free them to be secure, well-adjusted adults. The "needy" child still lives within and surfaces inappropriately at times, much to the dismay of the adult who "knows better." Adult temper tantrums, jealous insecurities, and other out-of-control behavior has its roots in unresolved childhood conflicts.

The results of dysfunctional families surround us: record highs for divorce, teen pregnancy, and drug and child abuse with its devastating effects. How to avoid those pitfalls is a priority with most couples, who vow not to repeat the mistakes of their parents with their own children. But it's easier said than done.

> **"My greatest hope is to raise a responsible, caring and intelligent individual, and be the best father possible."**

If you came from a dysfunctional family, you lack healthy role models to guide you. Without the appropriate tools and guidelines for change, mistakes are bound to be repeated or new ones introduced, even with the best of intentions. Consider the classic case of the new dad who comes from a family that had rules and regulations which stretched from here to Tibet. The atmosphere was restrictive and very regimented. This dad decides that he won't have all those rules to stifle his child, so he adopts a parenting style that's very liberal and permissive, with few rules. Those rules that do exist are largely ignored by the child as he realizes that dad can't say no, use effective discipline, or set limits. This child never learns respect for others or the valuable lesson of experiencing the consequences of his actions. The inmates end up running the asylum, and everyone suffers. As they say, "Two wrongs don't make a right." The key to parenting, as in everything else in life, is balance, a healthy balance between love and limits.

> **"My greatest fear for fatherhood is that I'll not be intimate with the child, not show or tell the baby how much I love him/her. My dad never did. My greatest hope would be to not follow his example.**

POSITIVE PARENTING

The suggested first step to being a healthy, positive parent is to do some thoughtful soul-searching. Take a look back into your own childhood and identify the emotional residue that will hinder your parenting abilities. We all have childhood issues with one or both parents that would be very beneficial to resolve. You don't want any loose ends from your childhood tripping you up with your own kids. As Dr. Bradshaw points out, "If you don't let it out, you act it out." You're doomed to repeat the negative patterns you learned in your family. By identifying and resolving your childhood issues, you can avoid repeating the pattern with your own children. You don't have to spend years on a psychiatrist's couch to do this. Various excellent books, videos, and groups can help you clarify where you are and how you can get where you want to be; see the Recommended Resources.

STRAIGHT SCOOP

Clear, nonthreatening, supportive communication that enhances understanding and conflict resolution is the key to healthy relationships, but there's a major stumbling block to realizing this kind of communication between the sexes. Men and women have different patterns and perceptions of communicating. Deborah Tannen, author of *You Just Don't Understand,* explains the reason for the difficulty in communication between couples. Women view talking as a way to relate, connect, and relax, but men view it as competition, negotiating status, and preserving independence. One sex uses it as a way to intimacy, the other as a way to keep distance. No wonder it can be so difficult getting on the same wave-length!

> **"It was a very volatile time. We fought about things we had never fought about before."**

NAME THAT FEELING

Another variable to blocked communication is the emotional factor. Observational researchers have found women to be more comfortable with verbal conflict as a means of resolving issues. They're not as threatened by emotional issues, whereas men react very physically to such verbal interactions. It's common for a man to withdraw and feign disinterest when confronted, but in actuality, he experiences conflict on a more gut level than a woman. Men suffer more physiological distress to the point of fright and flight response, and they take much longer to recover from such confrontations than women do.

While failure to identify feelings certainly isn't confined to the male sex, men have more of a problem simply because they aren't taught how to do that comfortably as children. This is really a problem for those men who learned their childhood lessons well. "Big boys don't cry. Don't be a cry baby. Be a little man; that didn't hurt." After awhile, you're so busy stifling feelings, you even stop recognizing what they are when they come up, and eventually you aren't comfortable with even the more positive emotions.

Dr. Levant and John Kelly, in their book *Between Father and Child,* help you learn effective communications skills that get you on the right track with your kids from the beginning, but you don't wait until your baby is talking to practice and implement these techniques—you practice them on your wife! You rediscover how to identify the feeling so you can deal with it effectively. You learn how to really listen to not only what the other person is saying, and you recognize the feeling that goes with it as well. Men who participated in the seminars at the Fatherhood Project reported that they significantly improved their communication skills and relationships with their wives by using the techniques they learned.

Your child will learn communication and relationship skills from the example you and your wife provide as role models. If you come from a dysfunctional family, break the cycle. Give your children the kind of legacy you'll be proud to have them pass onto their children.

> **"Our communication has definitely improved during pregnancy."**
>
> **"When I have concerns, we set aside time specifically to talk about them. She's very responsive when I express them to her. Our emotional intimacy has been enhanced by pregnancy."**

Check your community for seminars and support groups for fathers if you feel you need more guidance to becoming the kind of father you want to be. There is help out there.

ΔΔΔ

10

POTENTIAL PROBLEMS

Most couples expect pregnancy to be the normal physiological event that it usually is. Most women sail through pregnancy with a glow on their cheeks and feel great, but approximately 15 percent of pregnant women experience problems. When complications occur, your pregnancy game plan has to be fine-tuned. It's not an easy adjustment to make. In addition to the great anxiety complications bring, your wife's self-esteem takes a nose dive. She'll probably feel she's failed somehow. Disappointment and anger are common emotions as you both struggle to deal with the unexpected events. Knowing the facts goes a long way to help you cope with whatever complication has beset you. You both need added emotional support and accurate information to deal effectively with the changes. Here's an overview of the common complications that can occur in pregnancy.

GESTATIONAL DIABETES

Approximately 1 to 4 percent of pregnant women develop the condition known as gestational diabetes. By the second trimester, the hormones of pregnancy inhibit the effectiveness of insulin in the body. The insulin-producing pancreas has to work harder to keep up with the increased demand. Most women manage to meet the increased demand, but when the supply side can't meet the increased demand, a temporary state of sugar intolerance (diabetes) results. Without adequate insulin, food can't be converted into available energy. It's analogous to having a well-stocked food storage room, but the door is locked and the key (insulin) is lost. The body can starve even with a room full of food simply because there's no access to it. In the diabetic state, sugar is unable to move from the blood into cells to nourish them and release energy to run the body.

Your baby's prime fuel is sugar. His mom's blood sugar crosses the placenta with great ease to nourish him as he grows and develops. With gestational diabetes, there's a chronic excess of sugar in the maternal blood that gravitates to the baby, which is one reason diabetics can have very large babies. Excessive size increases the incidence of birth injury, placental insufficiency, and cesarean birth. Fortunately, your baby doesn't run the increased risk of developing congenital anomalies since gestational diabetes doesn't develop until the second trimester after the organs are developed.

After birth, when the high levels of sugar are cut off, your baby can develop low blood sugar (hypoglycemia). He's used to producing large amounts of insulin to handle the excess sugar, and his system doesn't adapt that quickly to the reduced need for insuliin.

Simple Screening

Many experts believe that all pregnant women need to be screened for gestational diabetes at 24 to 28 weeks of pregnancy. The pregnant woman ingests the equivalent of 50 grams of sugar in a drink or a high carbohydrate meal; a blood sample is taken 1 to 2 hours later. Screening is a sound investment. With early detection and appropriate management, many of the potential problems for both mom and baby can be avoided.

Treatment Techniques

Treatment of gestational diabetes is fairly simple. A diet from the American Diabetic Association controls blood sugar keeping it within safe limits. Mom and baby get the right amount of nutrients at the right times to keep mom's metabolism in balance. Scrupulous adherence to the diet helps prevent the problems of a too-large baby by keeping her mom's blood sugar within normal limits. A moderate exercise program also helps control blood sugar. If blood sugar can't be controlled with diet and exercise alone, insulin for the duration of the pregnancy will also be prescribed.

If your wife starts to feel down about having to go this extra mile in pregnancy, remind her that this metabolic condition is only temporary. Since the ADA diet is healthy for *everyone*, keep her company—it'll be easier for her to stick to it if you join her. It's worth a little extra effort to ensure that your baby will be healthy.

After Delivery

Fortunately, **g**estational diabetes is a temporary condition. After delivery, when the pregnancy hormones are gone, a woman's body is once again able to produce adequate insulin to meet her needs. Half the women who develop gestational diabetes during pregnancy are at increased risk for diabetes in later life, so follow-up care and evaluation by an internist or diabetologist is needed after pregnancy. Developing diabetes in later life is associated with a family history of the disease, obesity, lack of exercise, and faulty diet. After pregnancy, resolve to continue the good eating habits you both learned from the ADA diet, and continue exercising to lose unhealthy pounds. Those healthy habits will pay off in the future for your whole family.

INSULIN DEPENDENT DIABETES

There is also good news for the insulin-dependent diabetic who's contemplating pregnancy. With well-controlled sugar levels before and during pregnancy, the chances for having a healthy baby are better than ever.

Management of insulin-required diabetes in pregnancy has become more efficient, less costly, and less disruptive than it used to be. Home monitoring has revolutionized the management of diabetes. The instant and consistent feedback from home self-monitoring helps balance insulin and sugar needs and keeps levels within safe limits, which is particularly important during pregnancy.

To assure the best outcome possible for your planned baby, your wife should consult her internist, obstetrician, or perinatologist **before** she gets pregnant. Achieving the best control possible before conception lowers the risks for congenital anomalies. By the time she realizes she's pregnant, it may be too late since the anomalies occur in the first trimester. **The best prevention is before conception.**

HERPES

In the 80s, herpes simplex stopped being just a plain old cold sore and doused desire in many a sexual revolutionary. While no one longs for the good old days, the herpes hysteria from back then seems almost quaint in the face of AIDS in this decade. Here's a quick update on the current state of herpes as it relates to pregnancy.

Herpes complicates only 1 percent of pregnancies. The risks for pregnancy are with the primary (first) infection, not recurrences, which don't pose a problem for the baby. In early pregnancy with a primary infection, there's a greater risk for miscarriage. Birth deformities aren't a cause for concern; very rarely does the virus cross the placenta to the baby.

In the last 6 weeks of pregnancy, the risk for preterm labor and infecting the baby after birth increases. The number of babies who actually become infected with herpes after birth is very small, one in 4000 or 5000. Those babies who acquire herpes have a mortality rate of 40 percent. Two thirds of those who survive have serious neurological problems or eye damage. Here are a few simple guidelines to follow during pregnancy:

- If your wife has already been proven to have herpes, no cultures are needed during pregnancy.

- If you have herpes and your wife doesn't, her doctor needs to know. You may have to wear condoms during intercourse for the duration of the pregnancy to protect the baby and your wife.

- If your wife experiences a first occurrence, she needs to be cultured while the virus is still "shedding," or the first or second day after the outbreak. She needs to show her doctor exactly where her suspected lesion is located. *A culture is the only way to positively confirm if it's truly herpes.*

- During outbreaks, avoid spreading the lesions to other parts of the body by using good old soap and water as disinfectants. Corn starch on the sores and drying them with a hair dryer work as well as anything.

- The goal is to keep the baby and the virus separate. If lesions are present when labor begins, a cesarean birth may be necessary, but even with active lesions, more than 90 percent of babies don't become infected.

- If no lesions are detected at the time of labor, a vaginal birth is considered the best course.

It's not uncommon for a woman with herpes to feel the guilt and shame all over again when she gets pregnant. Your wife will need extra reassurance and support from you to work through it and not let it spoil this happy time in her life and yours.

PREECLAMPSIA

Preeclampsia, also known as toxemia, pregnancy-induced hypertension, or EPH gestosis, affects about 5 percent of pregnancies. It's history is long on myth and short on facts. The most important fact to remember is that **there's no known prevention for preeclampsia; the only cure is delivery of the baby.**

MORE FACTS

- Although the term *toxemia* is still used, it's not accurate because the disease isn't caused by a diseased placenta, poisons, or toxins in the body.

- Preeclampsia isn't the result of obesity or excessive weight gain during pregnancy.

- Salt (sodium chloride) doesn't cause preeclampsia. **Salt restriction won't cure or prevent the disease.** Normal amounts of salt should remain in the pregnant woman's diet.

- "Water pills" (diuretics) shouldn't be taken for any swelling.

- Preeclampsia isn't prevented by either vitamin therapy or high-protein or other special diets.

In addition to the first-time mother, women with diabetes, chronic hypertension, and multiple pregnancies are at risk for developing the disease. The mom's immunological computer, because of some unknown variable, doesn't "program" her response to the pregnancy in a normal way and preeclampsia results. Preeclampsia is dangerous for both mother and baby.

With this disease, the vascular system is altered. The blood vessels become alternately constricted and dilated, somewhat like a sausage. Blood flow is restricted as pressure increases within the vessel walls, and fluid is forced out into the tissues. Blood becomes thicker without the fluid. The blood pressures rises, and the changes in the vessels produce the three symptoms used to diagnose preeclampsia: edema (generalized swelling), hypertension (increased blood pressure), and protein in the urine (proteinuria).

With the decrease in blood volume and flow, the placenta delivers less oxygen and nutrients to the baby. The result can be a small baby who doesn't reach potential physical growth potential. Intrauterine growth retardation (IUGR) is the medical term used to describe the condition.

Subtle Symptoms

The first sign of preeclampsia is usually a weight gain of more than 2 pounds in 1 week. Generalized swelling (edema) appears next. While swelling of the feet and ankles is considered normal in pregnancy, swelling of the face and fingers isn't. If your wife's face becomes fuller and she can't get her rings off, she needs to call her doctor.

Treatment—Buying Time

Since delivery is the only cure for preeclampsia, the doctor tries to slow the progress of the disease until the baby's lungs are mature enough so the baby can be safely delivered. There aren't any advantages to waiting if it isn't necessary because the disease does not get better with time.

If your wife has mild preeclampsia, her doctor may let her stay at home and take her own blood pressure several times a day and rest while lying on her left side most of the time. This position relieves the pressure from the large vessels and allows the fluid to shift back into the vessels. Often the blood pressure will also decrease. Preeclampsia is very tricky; it can be mild in the morning but severe by evening. It must be watched very closely, and the doctor's orders for rest must be followed conscientiously. Cooking, cleaning, shopping, and chasing kids around are strictly off limits. Many women don't feel sick with this disease, so they're tempted to try and carry on as usual. If normal activities are continued, the preeclampsia will only get worse, and hospitalization will be required. Encourage your wife to follow her doctor's orders. Take off from work, if necessary, to help out, or hire someone to take over so she can get the rest she must have to keep the disease from getting worse.

Blood tests may be done weekly to monitor the progress of the disease. Ultrasound exams may be performed to reassure everyone that your baby is growing on schedule. The big danger with preeclampsia is the threat of convulsions. If your wife isn't getting better in spite of the decreased activity, hospitalization may be necessary.

After delivery, preeclampsia disappears as mysteriously as it appeared. Even women who have been very ill with the disease make a full recovery.

PRETERM LABOR

Six to eight percent of all babies born arrive before 37 weeks' gestation. While the numbers are small, these babies account for 75 percent of all the neonatal deaths—a significant statistic. It costs as much to care for 5 preterm babies as it does 150 pregnant women. Mother nature still provides the best incubator. There's no disagreement that preterm babies are best left in utero as opposed to the neonatal intensive care unit (NICU). Easier said than done.

The cause of 50 to 60 percent of preterm labors is unknown . You can't cure something if you don't know the cause. The best medicine can do at this point is to try and identify in advance those women most at risk for preterm labor. Here's a list of those factors that put a woman at risk for preterm labor.

Risk Factors for Preterm Labor

Major Factors
Previous preterm labor
Multiple pregnancy (twins or more)
Abdominal surgery during pregnancy
Two second trimester abortions
Cervix less than 1 cm long
Cervix dilated more than 1 cm
DES daughter (her mother was given diethylstilbesterol while pregnant to avoid miscarriage which caused uterine abnormalities in the baby).
Cone biopsy of cervix
Incompetent cervix
Irritable uterus
Polyhydramnios (excessive amniotic fluid)
Uterine anomaly (double uterus)

Minor factors
Bleeding after 12 weeks' in pregnancy
One abortion in the second trimester
Three or more first trimester elective abortions
Febrile (fever) illness
Pyelonephritis (kidney infection)
Smoking more than 10 cigarettes per day

Early diagnosis of preterm labor offers the best chance for sucess because once the cervix has started to dilate, it's difficult to stop the progress of labor for very long, even with the drugs now available. Teaching those women who are identified as high risk how to assess themselves for signs of uterine activity is one method used to decrease the incidence of preterm labor. The education is reinforced by frequent telephone contact with nurses who provide additional support and information.

Home monitoring is an investigational technique that may help identify preterm labor. A uterine contraction monitor is worn several times a day to record any uterine activity. The information is transmitted by phone to a central unit where the strip is evaluated. Some feel that the home monitoring system is both promising and effective; others feel that the combination of education, self-assessment by the pregnant woman, and frequent nurse contact works as well. (It's also less expensive). Time will tell.

Signs and Symptoms

The signs and symptoms of preterm labor are often very vague, confusing, and subtle since they mimic many of the usual aches and pains of pregnancy. Preterm labor may go unrecognized until the cervix has dilated. Suspect preterm labor if your wife has:

- Four or more noticeable, painless tightenings (contractions) of her uterus in 1 hour or less

- Dull aching cramps above the pubic bone. The cramps may come and go or be continuous

- Low backache different from the type she usually has, and changing position doesn't relieve it

- Feeling of pressure in the pelvis that comes and goes or is constant

- Any change or an increase in amount, consistency, or color (brown to pink) of her usual clear, mucusy, vaginal discharge

Urinary tract infections are a common cause of preterm labor symptoms. Call your wife's doctor if she has one or more symptoms (frequency and burning on urination). It's easier to deal with false alarms emotionally and financially than a preterm baby in the NICU for a month or two.

When in Doubt

If your wife experiences what she thinks are preterm labor symptoms, have her lie on her side and drink a quart of water. The combination of rest and fluids often quiets the irritable uterus. See Chapter 13, "Labor and Birth" for how to evaluate the strength, frequency, and duration of her contractions. If the contractions occur four or more times in an hour and she is less than 37 weeks' pregnant, she may be in preterm labor. Call her doctor. Tell her how often the contractions are occurring and what has already done to decrease the uterine activity.

Timely Treatment

If contractions continue in spite of your interventions, hospitalization is required for further observation and possible treatment of preterm labor. Fifty percent of women will respond to bed rest on the left side and an IV to increase their fluid level (hydration). The fetal monitor is used to evaluate uterine activity and how the baby is doing. If the contractions continue and the cervix is changing, the decision to try to stop labor has to be made. Labor usually won't be stopped if the

- Pregnancy is 35 weeks or more

- Baby's lungs are mature

- Cervix is 4 or more centimeters dilated

- Bag of waters has ruptured

Fetal distress, poorly controlled diabetes, severe preeclampsia, intrauterine infection, and bleeding are all considered contraindications to suppressing labor.

Overcoming Adversity

The birth of a preterm baby is a major crisis emotionally and financially. You both need all the love and support you can get. A hospital chaplain or social worker can help you with the emotional trauma and adjustments. The doctors and nurses in the NICU can help you cope with your new, fragile baby while you work through your grieving and bonding process at the same time. It's a lot to deal with. Don't try to muddle through on your own. There are lots of people who can help—let them.

TWINS

Twins occur once in every 100 pregnancies. Whether you're daunted by the prospect or delighted, the twin pregnancy needs extra attention. Before ultrasound, as many as 30 percent of twin pregnancies were surprises. Smelling salts were kept in the delivery room for just such special occasions. An ultrasound exam in early pregnancy can eliminate any surprises because you can see two babies in there—no guessing.

Twins may double your fun after birth, but there are potential problems during pregnancy that need to be anticipated. The twin pregnancy is considered high risk. The following list of potential problems gives you a good idea of why your wife's doctor is following the pregnancy so closely.

Potential Problems for Twin Pregnancy

- Significantly higher infant mortality rates than single pregnancies

- Low birthweights

- Preterm labor; twins deliver on the average about 3 weeks early

- Discordant growth—intrauterine sibling rivalry; one twin receives more nourishment from the placenta, and the other one is "underfed"

- Preeclampsia

- Maternal anemia

- Placental problems such as premature separation and placenta previa

- Complicated labor—if one twin is breech, a cesarean birth is often done

Several important things can be done to help your twins before birth:

- At about 28 to 32 weeks, the doctor may ask your wife to quit work and spend much of her time lying on her side to increase placental blood flow, which also helps your babies gain weight.

- Pay attention to any signs of preterm labor.

- Don't hesitate to **call the doctor if you suspect preterm labor.**

- Eat a well balanced diet with adequate calories.

- Take vitamins—the ones with the iron and folic acid are a good idea.

Several ultrasound exams will be done during pregnancy to follow the growth patterns of both babies to be sure they're both growing appropriately. Nonstress testing (discussed in the next chapter) might be added weekly at 32 weeks, if it's indicated, to evaluate how well the placenta is taking care of the babies.

The doctor will want your babies to be delivered in a hospital with equipment and personnel trained to care for babies like yours, especially if problems such as preterm labor strike. Discuss the options with the doctor. If preterm labor strikes, a level 2 or perinatal center is usually your best bet if the babies are under 33 weeks" gestation. See Health Care Options and Personnel section later in this chapter. It's less anxiety provoking if plans are made to provide for all possible developments.

BLOOD INCOMPATIBILITY

Rh Disease

Rh disease, also known as erthyroblastosis fetalis, is the result of blood incompatibility between the mother and her fetus. This disease used to be much more prevalent and posed great risks for the baby. There are only certain combinations of blood types that you need to worry about.

When the mom's blood type is negative and the baby's father's type is positive, the baby has a 50/50 chance of being positive too. If the baby is positive, there's a potential problem. The mother's body normally views the baby as a friendly, harmless parasite. In the Rh negative mom whose baby is Rh positive, the baby is viewed as an intruder. The mom's body takes aggressive action against the baby's system. She becomes sensitized and develops antibodies (weapons) to destroy the red blood cells in the baby. As the red blood cells are being destroyed, the baby becomes anemic. More problems develop as the baby tries compensating for the anemia. In severe cases, the fetal heart and liver can fail from trying to keep up, although with current treatment 70 percent of even severely affected babies survive.

Preventing Problems

Prevention is always the best approach, particularly so in this situation. Once the mother is sensitized, the sensitivity is lifelong and irreversible. There's no undoing once it's done

MOM	and	DAD →	BABY →	RESULT
(NEG)	and	(POS) →	(POS) →	**Potential Problem**
(NEG)	and	(POS) →	(NEG) →	**no problem**
(POS)	and	(NEG) →	(POS) →	**no problem**
(POS)	and	(NEG) →	(NEG) →	**no problem**
(POS)	and	(POS) →	(POS) →	**no problem**
(NEG)	and	(NEG) →	(NEG) →	**no problem**

Blood typing, Rh determination, and antibody screening are routinely done at the first prenatal visit. For Rh negative mothers, the antibody screen is repeated at 28 weeks' of pregnancy. If the mother isn't sensitized, an injection of Rh immune globulin (RhIG) is given to provide protection. After delivery, if the baby's blood type is positive, another injection of RhIG is given within 72 hours, to ensure protection. Even with tubal ligation, the RhIG is needed. Occasionally, tubal ligation fails, or at a later time the mother may want her tubes reconnected; better to cover all bases now.

Other Indications for RhIG

- Spontaneous abortion (miscarriage) occurring more than 6 weeks after the last menstrual period

- Induced abortion

- Ectopic pregnancy

- After amniocentesis

The RhIG injections, provide a good chance of eradicating Rh disease in our lifetime.

OVERDUE—POSTDATES PREGNANCY

If your wife goes 2 weeks past her due date she's considered postdates. By this time, she won't be happy camper or a good sport. She's long past being thrilled with pregnancy. She wants it over with—now.

Her doctor shares her feelings, but not for the same reasons. The doctor's concern is about the "aging" placenta being able to still provide enough oxygen and nutrients to your baby. There are other factors to weigh in order to make the appropriate decisions about the best time for delivery.

If the cervix is unripe, many doctors prefer to leave well enough alone, as long as the fetal well-being tests are reassuring, the baby is growing appropriately, and there's an adequate amount of amniotic fluid. An unripe cervix decreases the chances of a successful induction of labor. Sometimes it works, sometimes not. With an unripe cervix, it may take several days of trying to finally get labor going.

When the cervix is ripe, most doctors feel comfortable inducing labor. Everybody can breathe a sigh of relief, and your wife may even start speaking to you again.

WHEN TO CALL THE DOCTOR
Vaginal Bleeding

Vaginal bleeding doesn't always mean problems with the pregnancy or danger to the baby, but it needs to be checked out. It's common for a pregnant woman to panic if she's on the toilet when she discovers any bleeding; even a few drops look like gallons when they hit the water. Help her keep calm and make note of the color: bright red or more reddish-brown? Is it coming from the vagina or rectum (she can check with some toilet paper)? Did the bleeding start after some activity, such as intercourse or physical activity? Does she have cramping or localized pain anywhere? The doctor will also want to know how much blood was actually lost. There's a difference between bleeding and hemorrhaging: If blood isn't running down her leg and filling her shoe, she isn't hemorrhaging. You don't have to call 911; keep calm and call her doctor.

94

Swollen Face and Fingers—Generalized Swelling

While swelling of feet and ankles is common in pregnancy, swelling of face and fingers isn't. Generalized swelling (face, fingers, feet, and ankles) may be a sign of preeclampsia (toxemia). Your wife needs to see her doctor.

Severe Or Continuous Headache

Although it's not an early or common symptom, headache that's severe or continuous is a possible sign of preeclampsia. Dimness or blurring of vision may accompany this type of headache. Migraine headaches also show these symptoms.

Abdominal Pain

Aches and pains are so common in pregnancy that it's difficult to decide if abdominal pain is something to be concerned about. Before calling the doctor, decide what kind of pain she's having. Where is it? What does it feel like? Does she have any other symptoms besides abdominal pain, such as bleeding? Has she noticed an increase in her usual vaginal discharge? Does the pain come and go, or is it constant? It may just be the old round ligament pain again, or it may be something significant such as preterm labor. Call her doctor and check it out.

Persistent Vomiting

Such vomiting is usually associated with a more severe form of morning sickness called hyperemesis gravidarium that goes beyond the usual 12 to 16 weeks' of pregnancy. Severe attacks of flu can also produce uncommon vomiting. The danger with persistent vomiting is dehydration to the point of upsetting the body's chemical balance. Don't let your wife wait until she's severely dehydrated to call her doctor. If she waits too long, she may have to be hospitalized for fluid-replacement therapy:IVs.

Chills or Fever

Your wife could have the old garden variety flu that resolves itself in 24 to 48 hours or so, but she could also have a kidney infection, which is serious. If her temperature is over 101 degrees, call her doctor. If she has a fever lower than 101 degrees but pain in the kidney area and/or frequency and burning on urination, notify her doctor; she may have a kidney infection.

If she has typical flu with temperatures below 101 degrees and no other symptoms, she can take Tylenol and drink fluids. If the symptoms don't resolve within 24 hours, or she has questions, consult her doctor.

Painful Urination

Most women don't have to be talked into calling the doctor for this one. With this infection, your wife feels like her bladder is going to explode, but she's able to pass only a few drops that feel like razor blades as they trickle reluctantly down her urethra. A bladder infection, besides being very painful, is a common cause of preterm labor symptoms and needs to be treated because it doesn't cure itself. The doctor can give your wife medication to alleviate the painful urination and another one to knock out the infection.

Accidental Injury

Generally, the baby is well protected from blunt trauma to the abdomen in early and middle pregnancy by the cushioning effect of the amniotic fluid. In late pregnancy, injury to the baby is more likely to occur when the head is fixed in the pelvis and amniotic fluid is normally decreased.

Seven percent of women experience some type of injury during pregnancy, but the vast majority of these accidents don't harm the baby. Occasionally, injury to the abdomen can seriously decrease oxygen to the baby. Premature separation of the placenta from the uterine wall and the high stress levels associated with an automobile accident or other trauma can be contributing factors.

If your wife is involved in an accident and experiences a blow to her abdomen, notify her doctor, who may want to order some tests to reassure everyone that the baby hasn't been affected. A fetal monitor and a contraction stress test can detect signs of fetal distress. The Kleihauer-Betke blood test is done to detect fetal bleeding. The tests may take 2 or 3 hours to complete, but you'll both have some peace of mind.

An ounce of prevention: She must wear her three point seat belt restraint. The lap belt should be positioned on her thighs. Seat belts significantly decrease injury to both mom and baby.

AVAILABLE HEALTH CARE OPTIONS AND PERSONNEL
Health Care

With a complicated pregnancy, you need to be aware of the different health care options available. Many states classify hospitals according to the level of services they are able to provide:

A *level 1* center is usually a small community hospital that offers basic obstetrical services to the woman with a low-risk pregnancy. Such a hospital isn't equipped to handle mothers with complications such as preterm labor, severe preeclampsia, diabetes, or babies who need more sophisticated care.

A *level 2* center offers services to the low-risk mother and complicated pregnancies. They have a neonatal intensive care unit (NICU) to care for babies who are preterm or have medical problems.

The *level 3* center is the designated perinatal center for the region. The perinatal center has perinatologists, neonatologists, and the necessary trained personnel to care for the very high-risk mother and her baby. All necessary services are offered on a 24-hour basis, including genetic counseling, maternal/fetal transport, education, and research. While a level 3 center specializes in high-risk care, they usually offer services to the low-risk mother as well.

Personnel

Obstetricians specialize in caring for the pregnant woman. A board-certified obstetrician is one who has passed a rigorous written and verbal examination by a board of peers from the American College of Obstetricians and Gynecologists. A doctor is eligible to take the exam after being in obstetrical practice for 3 years. The certificate is not required to practice, but it's considered a badge of honor— going the extra mile to demonstrate competence.

Perinatologists are obstetricians with added training. They specialize in the care of complicated and very high-risk pregnancies, such as women with diabetes requiring insulin. Most of the time, perinatologists are located in perinatal centers. Their practice base is mainly referral from obstetricians. In addition to direct care of the high risk mother, they provide consultation services to the obstetrician if they are needed.

Neonatologists are pediatricians with added expertise who specialize in the care of the new baby with medical problems or conditions that require intensive care such as the very preterm baby. Neonatologists work closely with highly skilled and trained nurses in the NICU to provide the highest quality care available for the baby who needs it.

When you're investigating hospitals in which to deliver, ask if they're a level 1, 2, or 3 for future reference. For instance, if your wife is a diabetic who requires insulin, a Level 1 center wouldn't be able to provide the services you need.

ΔΔΔ

11

FETAL TESTS

When complications, such as the ones discussed in Chapter 10 occur during pregnancy, certain tests will provide important information. In many cases, the information can reassure everyone that the baby is doing well in spite of the complication. If the information indicates that the baby is in jeopardy, the doctor can decide how best to proceed for both mother and baby's sake. The various tests currently used to assess the fetus at risk are discussed in this chapter. Keep in mind that while the tests are immensely helpful to your doctor, they aren't foolproof.

STRESS AND NONSTRESS TESTS

These two tests determine if the baby is receiving enough oxygen and nutrients from the placenta. They provide a way for the baby to tell us if he is receiving adequate supplies necessary for his well-being, or if he's having difficulty making ends meet. When the placenta is unable to supply the necessities, the decision has to be made as to when to deliver the baby to a more friendly environment outside the uterus.

Contraction Stress Test (CST)
Oxytocin Challenge Test (OCT)

Oxytocin is a natural female hormone that stimulates the uterus to contract. While the uterus contracts, the flow of oxygen to the baby is temporarily decreased, similar to the effect of you holding your breath. A healthy baby with normal oxygen reserves has no problems coping with the temporary decrease, but the chronically deprived baby will show subtle, detectable changes in his heart rate with even a temporary decrease in oxygen flow.

Both the CST and OCT are the equivalent of intrauterine physical fitness tests. They evaluate placental function. The baby's heart rate is observed and evaluated through three contractions occurring in a 10-minute period. The fetal monitor records and evaluates any changes in the baby's heart rate that may indicate potential problems with oxygenation.

With the CST, the oxytocin is released through self-stimulation of the maternal nipples by rubbing or rolling. While this method is less expensive than the OCT, it's only successful about 75 percent of the time.

With the OCT, oxytocin is administered through an IV line placed in the hand or wrist. The medication is increased until 3 contractions in a 10-minute period are produced. If the baby isn't distressed by the intermittent lack of oxygen during the contractions, the test is called "negative." It's a reassuring sign that the baby can remain inside for another week. If the test is "positive,"the baby shows signs of distress; the doctor will want to discuss the best options available for your situation.

The contractions produced by either method are painless. The OCT may take 1 hour to complete. Once the stimulation or medication is discontinued, the contractions subside within an hour in most cases. The chances of initiating actual labor are very remote. Testing usually begins at 34 weeks' of pregnancy and continues weekly until delivery.

Nonstress Test—NST

The NST evaluates the baby's central nervous system. If the baby's central nervous system is able to function normally by raising her heart rate when stimulated, it's a reassuring sign that adequate oxygen is being supplied from the placenta. The fetal monitor identifies the relationship between the baby's movements and accelerations of the heart rate. If the baby moves at least twice in 20 minutes and the heart rate accelerates by 15 beats for 15 seconds above the baseline pulse, the test is referred to as "reactive." It's reassuring that the baby is currently doing well. When a test is "nonreactive," an OCT is usually done to further evaluate the heart rate by testing placental function.

Nonstress testing is done weekly or biweekly at about 34 weeks in pregnancy and continues until the baby is delivered. The NST is less complicated and costly to perform and can be done in the doctor's office. No medication or IV is required.

Common Indications for Stress and Nonstress Testing

- Maternal diabetes (insulin needed)
- Preeclampsia (toxemia)
- Chronic hypertension
- RH disease
- Previous stillborn
- Postdates pregnancy (more than 2 weeks overdue)
- Maternal cardiac disease
- Maternal hyperthryroidism
- Intrauterine growth retardation (IUGR)

BIOPHYSICAL PROFILE

With the biophysical profile, ultrasound is used to evaluate fetal movements, breathing motions, baby's muscle tone, and the amount of amniotic fluid present. Fetal heart rhythm and reactivity are also evaluated with the nonstress test. The biophysical profile and the additional data it provides is an important assessment tool for the doctor when the OCT or NST results may be unclear.

FETAL ACOUSTIC STIMULATION (FAS) TEST

Instead of contractions, a vibratory device that produces a sound at 80 decibels is applied to the mother's abdomen for 3 seconds to evaluate the reactivity of the baby. A baby with a healthy central nervous system will be startled by the high-pitched sound and increase her heart rate in response. If she can accelerate her heart rate 15 beats per minute above her resting pulse twice within 10 minutes for at least 15 seconds, the test is considered reactive and reassuring.

PRENATAL GENETIC TESTING

A number of genetic disorders can be detected by amniotic fluid analysis and/or chorionic villus sampling. These disorders include Duchenne muscular dystrophy, alpha and beta thalassemia, hemophilia, sickle cell anemia, cystic fibrosis, and polycystic kidney disease.

You and your wife can use the Prenatal Genetic Questionnaire in Appendix 2, adapted from and developed by the American College of Obstetricians and Gynecologists, to see if your baby might be at risk for any of the disorders listed. If you discover any risk factors, discuss them with your doctor.

AMNIOCENTESIS

With ultrasound as a guide, 1/2 to 1 ounce of amniotic fluid is withdrawn from one of the pockets of amniotic fluid that surround the baby. The ultrasound makes the procedure much less risky because the doctor can see precisely where the baby, placenta, umbilical cord, and pockets of fluid are located.

Local anesthetic injected to numb the skin makes the procedure fairly painless. Most women report feeling pressure as the longer needle goes in, but not pain. The procedure takes 10 to 15 minutes to complete.

After the amniocentesis, intermittent cramping is a common occurrence, but the cramping usually subsides within a couple of hours. Occasionally, a small amount of amniotic fluid leaks from the vagina, but the leak quickly seals over. There's no harm to the baby since new amniotic fluid is manufactured all the time. If the leaking should continue, your wife's doctor needs to be called. In the meantime, she should avoid douching, intercourse, and use of tampons until her doctor can evaluate the leaking.

The complication rate for amniocentesis is 1 percent—*extremely low*. The risks for preterm labor, or sticking the baby, cord, or placenta with the needle are very remote, particularly when used with ultrasound. Amniocentesis is a widely used and important diagnostic tool. Here are the common indications for amniocentesis.

Common Uses for Amniocentesis

Genetic Studies—Analysis of amniotic fluid detects inherited diseases such as Tay-Sachs syndrome or chromosome disorders such as Down's syndrome (mongolism). Amniocentesis can't be done until 15 to 18 weeks, at which time there is sufficient amniotic fluid for a specimen.

Neural Tube Defects—Deformities of the spinal cord such as spina bifida (spinal cord not covered) and anencephaly (deformed head with exposed brain) can be confirmed. See the Serum Alpha Fetoprotein section.

Fetal Lung Maturity— When the due date is uncertain, or preterm labor threatens, amniotic fluid analysis can determine if the baby can be safely delivered or if labor should be stopped until the baby's lungs can mature sufficiently to avoid problems.

Rh Disease—With this disease, there's an incompatibility between the mother and the baby's blood. Amniocentesis will show the amount of bilirubin (decomposed red blood cells) in the amniotic fluid. High rates of bilirubin may indicate a severely anemic baby that needs to be delivered. See the Rh disease section in Chapter 10.

CHORIONIC VILLUS SAMPLING (CVS)

CVS can detect certain genetic abnormalities as early as the ninth week of pregnancy. A small slim tube or catheter is directed into the cervix under ultrasound guidance. A small sample of the baby's placenta is then obtained for analysis. Results are available in approximately a week's time, which is a big advantage when anxiety levels are high. Since amniotic fluid isn't taken, the additional biochemical studies amniotic fluid offers can't be done with CVS alone.

The disadvantages of CVS over amniocentesis are a slightly higher infection and pregnancy loss rate. CVS isn't, at this time, widely available; only a few specially designed medical centers offer this service.

Serum alpha fetoprotein (AFP)

Maternal blood taken at 15 to 16 weeks of pregnancy can be evaluated for neural tube defects such as anencephaly or spina bifida, but even an elevated AFP level, doesn't automatically confirm anencephaly or spina bifida since a number of other conditions can produce the same elevation. AFP levels that are higher than normal are evaluated further with amniotic fluid analysis and ultrasound to confirm or rule out those abnormalities. AFP is a screening, not a diagnostic, test.

ULTRASOUND (USG)—WOMB WITH A VIEW

USG has provided a picture window for viewing the baby in the womb. It has removed a lot of guesswork regarding the fetus and his environment. The internal organs, placenta, and umbilical cord can be seen as well as movements such as the heart beating and the baby sucking his thumb.

USG operates the way sonar does in a submarine. Short pulses of intermittent, low-intensity sound waves are sent from the scanner placed on the mother's abdomen. As the sound waves "echo" off the baby, the signal is returned and converted into a picture of the baby on the screen. It's usually very exciting for anyone, especially the parents, to see the baby for the very first time.

How safe?

USG has been used for about 30 years and is considered safe. The risks are hypothetical, and well-controlled studies by reputable researchers report no evidence that USG has any ill effects on babies.

It's common for women to have at least 1 USG exam during pregnancy. The National Institute of Health (NIH) lists 27 approved uses for USG but doesn't endorse its use for bonding or determining the sex of the baby. If your doctor recommends an USG exam, you and your wife should know why the exam is necessary and what benefits or answers it will provide. You probably won't have to ask—most doctors are very happy to keep you informed.

Ultrasound has had the greatest impact on the practice of obstetrics of any diagnostic testing method in the last decade; those obstetricians who use USG in their practices couldn't imagine practicing without it. The following gives you a good idea of the different uses for ultrasound during pregnancy.

Uses for Ultrasound

First Trimester

Confirm pregnancy. if your wife is experiencing bleeding, USG can reassure everyone by seeing that your baby's heart is still beating. A tubal pregnancy can also be evaluated or ruled out.

Accurate dating of pregnancy. **USG** is often used to pinpoint the due date. In the first trimester, it can be accurate to within 1 week. It's an important baseline to establish if a previous pregnancy was complicated by cesarean birth, stillborn, small for dates baby, preterm labor, twins, high blood pressure, diabetes, kidney or heart disease. An accurate due date makes the decision for delivery decidedly easier.

Second Trimester

The due date can be calculated within one to two weeks if the USG is done at this time.

Genetic Counseling. If there's a family history of anomalies, or your wife will be 35 or over when she delivers, her doctor may recommend an amniocentesis for genetic studies. The amniocentesis may be done by either her doctor or a perinatologist at the nearest regional high-risk center. Chorionic villus sampling in the first trimester is also an option if it's available in your area.

Third Trimester

Measure fetal growth. If your baby is suspected of being small or large for the estimated due date, the pattern of growth can be evaluated by USG. Intrauterine growth retardation (IUGR), which refers to the baby's physical size and development, not mental development, can be ruled out. With IUGR, the placenta is unable to provide normal nutrition; the baby may be chronically underfed. If IUGR is diagnosed, the baby can be delivered early, if necessary.

Determine fetal position. If a breech presentation or other abnormal position is diagnosed, there's time to discuss and plan the best method of delivery.

Amniocentesis guide. It's essential to use USG as a guide to minimize the risks of the amniocentesis procedure. The procedure may be done in the doctor's office or the hospital under ultrasound guidance.

MAGNETIC RESONANCE IMAGING (MRI)

Magnetic resonance imaging is the newest technology being used in obstetrics. MRI is safer than the old x-ray diagnostic studies. MRI provides data on fetal structure, development, and growth. MRI confirms fetal anomalies and visualizes maternal abdominal or pelvic structures when USG scanning isn't possible because of either obesity or gas.

It's normal to be very anxious when the doctor orders fetal tests. Before all-out anxiety takes over, be sure you really understand what the doctor is telling you. Discuss the circumstances until you're clear about what is really going on. If you don't understand something, say so. *The doctor doesn't want you to leave the office without the correct information or understanding.* Knowing the facts greatly reduces anxiety for both you and your wife. Many of the current tests can be greatly reassuring at a time when you need it most.

ΔΔΔ

▲▲▲▲▲▲▲▲▲▲▲▲ **PART 3** ▲▲▲▲▲▲▲▲▲▲▲▲

IMPLEMENTATION

▲▲▲▲▲▲▲▲▲▲▲▲▲▲▲▲▲▲▲▲▲▲▲▲

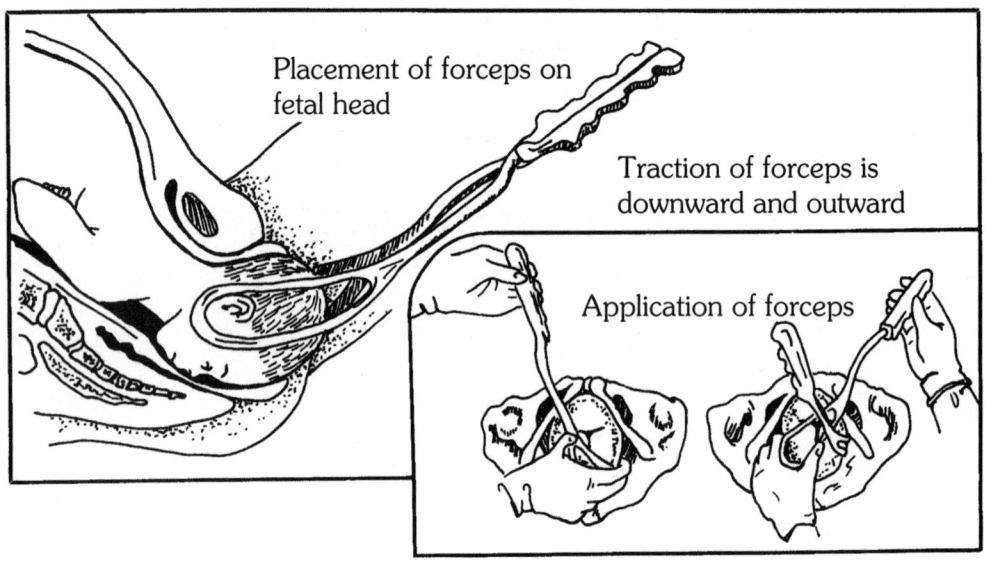

Placement of forceps on fetal head

Traction of forceps is downward and outward

Application of forceps

12

SPECIAL DELIVERY

Vaginal Birth

Forceps

Forcep deliveries have decreased dramatically in the last 20 years. The use of midforceps, with its increased risk for birth trauma, was largely abandoned because cesarean birth was safer for the baby. Because of the increased interest in natural childbirth, many women rejected regional anesthesia such as caudal, epidural, and spinal, so even low forceps were used less frequently. Currently, doctors are more willing to let the mother push for more than the traditional 2 hours. Also, labor nurses are more liberal in helping her push in different positions to help the baby move down more efficiently. Squatting or sitting, while pushing, often adds that extra little bit of space to the pelvic outlet so gravity can help move the baby down.

Low forceps do have a place in obstetrics. They can be very useful in the second stage of labor when, for example, there's evidence of fetal distress. Sometimes, after a long labor, the mother is just too exhausted to push and needs some help. When the baby's head is well down into the pelvis, a properly performed forceps delivery is not dangerous for the mother or baby. Anesthesia is required since the procedure is very uncomfortable for the mother. General or regional anesthesia (epidural or spinal) is used to provide good relief from pain.

Vacuum Extractor

Instead of forceps, some doctors prefer to use the vacuum extractor. A soft silicone cup is attached to the baby's head by suction. Gentle traction aids in delivering the baby's head. Unlike forceps, anesthesia isn't necessary with the vacuum extractor and it's no more uncomfortable than pushing. The baby's scalp swells at the site of the suction cup, but the swelling disappears in 24 hours.

CESAREAN BIRTH

Twenty-five years ago, the cesarean birthrate is this country was less than 5 percent; the current figure is 20 percent in most hospitals. What happened? Many people erroneously believe money is the main motivating factor, but that isn't the reason. A number of other factors have contributed to the dramatic increase.

The rise in the cesarean birthrate actually reflects some important changes in the attitudes and practice in obstetrics over the years. In past years, when couples had larger families, it was common for some babies to be lost during childbirth. The sad event was accepted and resolved as God's will, or fate. Doctor's weren't usually blamed or sued for malpractice. Now that couples are delaying childbearing and having fewer babies, they're much less accepting of less than perfect outcomes. If something goes wrong, somebody must be to blame, and somebody better pay. This attitude is reflected in the very dramatic increase in malpractice insurance coverage that's driving many obstetricians out of the field. The threat of a lawsuit puts the obstetrician in a more precarious position when labor doesn't progress normally or complications occur. In spite of the anxiety of a potential lawsuit, the majority of cesareans are done for very standard and legitimate reasons. Here are the usual indications and reasons for cesarean birth.

Routine Reasons

The three most common reasons for cesarean birth are contractions that lack sufficient force to dilate the cervix, a large baby, and the pelvic size of the mother.

One or all of these situations may work together to stall progress in labor and start talk of a cesarean.

Cephalopelvic disproportion (CPD) occurs when the baby is too big to fit through her mom's pelvis. Even with good contractions that should do the job, the baby is stuck at a certain point. The cervix refuses to dilate any further, and/or the baby doesn't move down the birth canal even when the cervix is fully dilated. A woman in labor is expected to dilate at the rate of 1 to 1-1/2 centimeters per hour. When her cervix stops dilatating after several hours, her doctor starts looking for answers. Failure to progress in labor can be due to CPD or ineffective uterine contractions. Before the diagnosis of CPD can be made, the doctor has to evaluate the strength of the uterine contractions. You can't do anything about CPD, but you can encourage stronger contractions to get the cervix dilating again if that's the problem. The most effective way to measure the strength of the contractions is to use an internal uterine catheter. If the contractions are measuring less than 50 millimeters of mercury (mmHg), they aren't doing the job. IV oxytocin is usually given to increase effective contractions so your baby can make an entrance before you're eligible for social security. Most women prefer not to have to resort to artificial means, but if you don't use the oxytocin, the only other alternative may be cesarean birth. Often, only very small doses of oxytocin are needed to finish the job. With small doses, the contractions are not more painful, as some people believe. Experts agree that more cesarean births could be avoided with closer evaluation of the situation when progress fails and by stimulating labor with oxytocin.

This is one of those situations in which you have to weigh your options. All the contributing factors in the situation should be discussed with you so you understand why the doctor chooses certain options over others. It should make perfect sense so you don't have any doubts. If you have both developed trust and rapport with her doctor, and your questions have been answered satisfactorily, you should feel comfortable with whatever decision is made.

The incidence of true CPD is undoubtedly much less than previously thought. Numerous studies have now demonstrated that half of women previously delivered by cesarean for CPD and/or failure to progress will deliver vaginally in a subsequent pregnancy if given a trial of labor. See the Vaginal Birth after Cesarean section in this chapter.

> **"I'm really worried about her having a long, long labor, or a breech position and having to have a C-section."**

Fetal Distress

In the old days the labor nurse listened to the baby's heartbeat once an hour for 15 seconds. It didn't provide much information aside from how fast or slow it was. Some cesareans were done for fetal distress that wasn't there, but many more babies who were distressed were missed because a stethoscope couldn't pick up the subtle clues.

In the early days of fetal monitoring, more cesareans were done for fetal distress, but now the diagnosis of fetal disress accounts for only a small percentage of the increase in the cesarean birthrate. Our knowledge of fetal monitoring and heart rate patterns has increased dramatically. Much is still to be learned, but more than a few cesareans have been avoided because the fetal heart rate pattern on the monitor was reassuring. In many cases, fetal monitoring allows health care personnel to head off disaster by detecting early signs of fetal distress.

Repeat Cesarean

The undisputed culprit in the dramatic increase in abdominal delivery is the repeat cesarean. In the past, it was believed that the uterine scar would separate during labor. "Once a cesarean, always a cesarean" was the rule of the day. Eventually, studies disproved that long-held belief. True CPD is rare, and the uterine scar is tougher than everybody thought.

Everyone agrees that the cesarean birthrate is too high, so various approaches are being examined to decrease the rate without increasing mortality and injury rates for the baby.

Heads Up—The Breech Baby

Three percent of babies are breech (head up and bottom down). With a vaginal birth, breech babies have a higher incidence of complications and neurological problems—some of those less than perfect outcomes. Most doctors recommend that all first babies, if breech, be delivered by cesarean since the complications and mortality of vaginal birth are higher in this group. Women who have already had one baby or more may be at less risk for problems since at least one baby has been through the birth canal. But not everyone agrees with this theory.

Some doctors are willing to attempt a vaginal delivery if certain criteria are met, but the decision shouldn't be made lightly. After eliminating various high-risk factors, such as double footling (feet first), large baby, and small pelvis, only 20 percent of breeches are acceptable candidates for a vaginal delivery. Such small numbers are not going to make a large impact on the cesarean birthrate.

A breech delivery is a dying art that requires loads of experience, great skill, and nerves of steel. Too many things can go wrong. Delivery can be blocked if the baby's arms become "locked" over her head. The cord can drop into the vagina before the body is delivered and cut off her oxygen. Things usually get very tense, especially as the doctor is trying to deliver the head, which must be done within very few minutes to avoid death from suffocation or brain damage from lack of oxygen. There's no turning back once the body is delivered, and you can't be sure how things will go until it's too late. It's not surprising why the standard of practice is to deliver breeches by cesarean instead of vaginally.

External Version—Bottoms Up

External version is an old trick of the trade making a comeback. External version is the procedure whereby the baby is turned from bottom down to head down. Near term, the pregnant abdomen can be manipulated externally to turn the baby into the normal position of head first.

The procedure involves some risk and expense. The umbilical cord can become entangled cutting of oxygen to the baby, and/or the placenta can separate

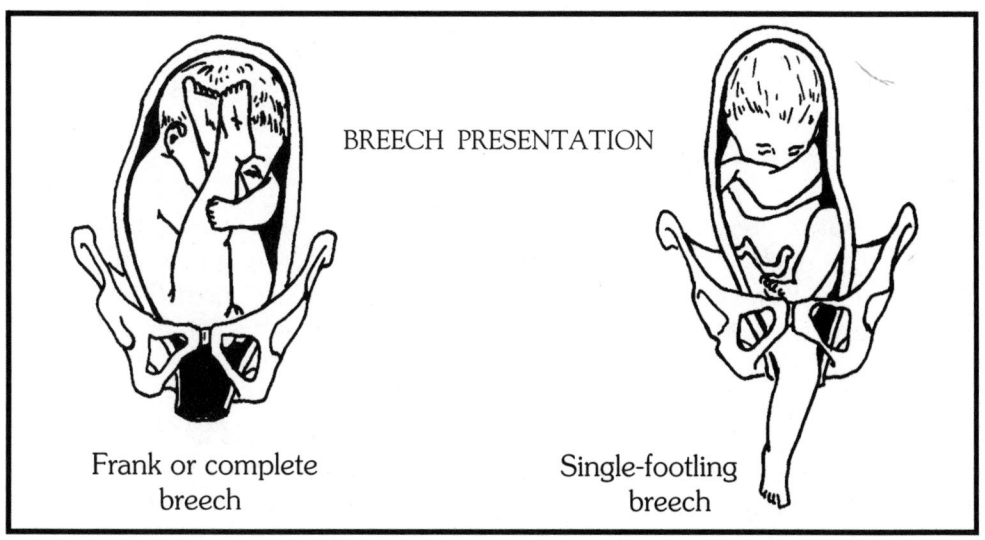

BREECH PRESENTATION

Frank or complete breech

Single-footling breech

from the uterine wall. The procedure is performed in the hospital for safety. Keep in mind that an emergency cesarean may have to be done for fetal distress if complications occur. External version requires a full ultrasound exam, fetal monitoring, IV with medication to relax the uterus, and the doctor to perform the manipulation. It can be expensive, so check to see if your insurance will cover the cost.

There is no guarantee the version will work, but the procedure is successful about 75 percent of the time. The success rate depends on the skill of the doctor and favorable circumstances—it's always worth a try.

New insights into safety factors gave birth to an option that will do the most to decrease the cesarean birth statistics—read on.

VAGINAL BIRTH AFTER CESAREAN—VBAC
Tough Incisions

Doctors have found a difference in the types of incisions used to open the uterus. The low transverse incision, made in the lower segment of the uterus, withstands the stress of uterine contractions very well. The incidence of uterine scar separation is half of 1 percent—extremely low—making it safe for a vaginal delivery the next time around. This is now the most commonly used incision for both the uterus and the skin incision referred to as the bikini cut. The bikini incision is less painful, heals better, rarely results in hernias, and keeps open your wife's options in swimwear.

The classical uterine incision (vertical—up and down) is often not strong enough to withstand labor. Nobody disagrees with this one; it's an automatic repeat cesarean. The classical incision may be used when the baby is lying transversely (sideways) or is preterm, or very large.

Once the safety of the low transverse uterine incision was established, it seemed reasonable to allow those women without a recurring problem such as breech or fetal distress to attempt a vaginal delivery if they so desired. Success rates were more than encouraging: two-thirds or more of the women delivered vaginally.

The American College of Obstetricians and Gynecologists encourages their members to be more liberal in performing VBAC. Hospitals have relaxed the previous rigid rules so doctors don't have to be present during the entire labor. More doctors are offering VBAC as an option. The VBAC rate could be still higher, but some women just don't want to go through labor and opt for another cesarean. Some doctors are still not comfortable with the whole idea of a trial of labor. It may take a few more years before VBAC can make a bigger dent in those cesarean birthrates.

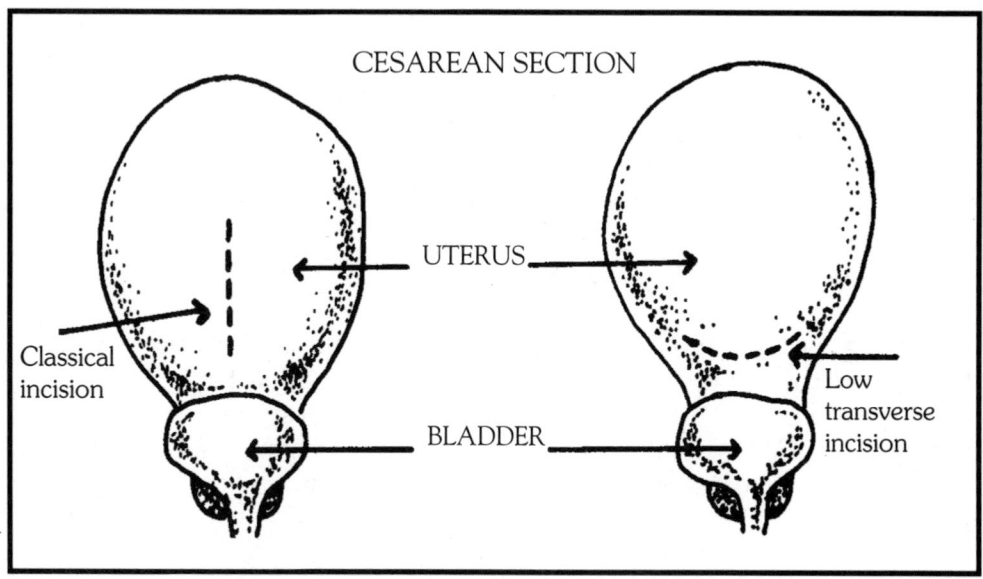

THIRTY SOMETHING

Obstetricians are reconsidering previous dire predictions for the pregnancy-after-35 group. In past years, obstetricians considered the mature gravida as obstetricially senescent, or, more to the point, over the hill. At that time, there weren't enough women in that age group to realistically evaluate the impact and outcomes for women opting to have babies at a later age. Times have changed. Now more women are currently in the 30 to35 and over age group than the 20 to 29 age group. The proportion of babies born to women 35 and over will double by the end of the century. The late bloomer has become the majority instead of an obstetrical oddity.

A New Look

How risky is it to have a baby these days if your wife is 35 or more?If she is 35 to 44 and *healthy*, here's what you can anticipate, based on recent studies. She has *no increased risk* for

- Preterm delivery
- Intrauterine growth retardation (IUGR)
- Low Apgar score baby
- Infant death

The risks during pregnancy *increase slightly* for:

- Gestational diabetes
- Preeclampsia
- Bleeding during pregnancy
- Placental abruption (bleeding from premature separation of the placenta)
- Placenta previa (low-lying placenta)

The cesarean birthrate is higher in the 35 and over mother, possibly due to the slight increase for pregnancy complications and a slightly higher incidence of fetal distress in labor. Plus, doctors may have a more conservative approach since the mature gravida has waited a long time for her baby. Doctors may be more willing to throw in the towel sooner with the more mature mother-to-be if labor isn't progressing.

Each year, after age 35, the risk for a baby with Down's syndrome (mongolism) increases. Here is the risk of Down's syndrome according to maternal age.

Maternal Age at Delivery	*Frequency of Down's Syndrome*
35	1/365
36	1/287
37	1/225
38	1/176
39	1/139
40	1/109
41	1/85
42	1/67
43	1/53
44	1/41

Women at age 35 are offered the option of an amniocentesis to detect Down's syndrome.

Closing Comments

Late bloomers seem highly motivated. In one study, they used less medication during labor and delivery, and more tended to breast-feed (95 percent) compared to 42 percent in other age groups.

If your wife has no health problems—such as high blood pressure, diabetes, kidney or heart disease, she's not high risk. There are no significant differences in outcomes in the 35 to 44 age group for either mom or baby. You can both relax and enjoy this special time in your life.

EMERGENCY DELIVERY

It doesn't happen very often, but some babies won't wait until mom and dad get to the hospital or birth center before making their grand entrance. We've all heard tales about taxicab drivers and firefighters delivering babies who were in a hurry. Here are some tips in case you find yourself in such an unlikely spot.

Designated Catcher

When babies come this fast, they can practically do it themselves. Here's what to do if you find yourself the catcher's seat:

- Have your wife lie down on a bed or the back seat of the car.

- **Remind her to use her breathing exercises and relax** between the contractions.

- **Don't leave her.** Let someone else call 911 for help.

- **Have her use the pant-blow breathing so she won't push.** The baby will ease out slowly. The side-lying position is easier for delivery and helps relax the perineum. If she wants to stay on her back, place something under her to elevate her hips.

- **Don't try to hold the baby back.** If the water bag is still intact, snag it with your finger, or a pin—it's just like breaking a water-filled balloon.

EMERGENCY DELIVERY GUIDE

If the water bag is still intact and bulging, break it with a pin or your finger. It looks like a water filled balloon.

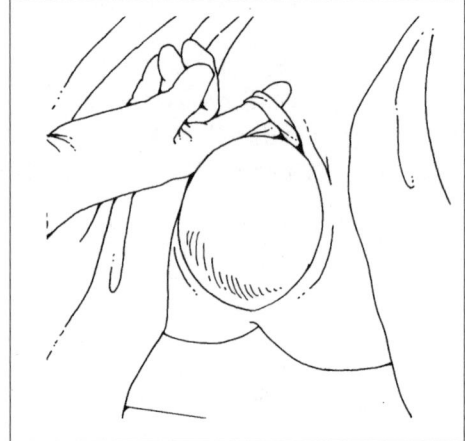

Run your fingers around the baby's neck to check for loops of cord. Pull the loops over his head.

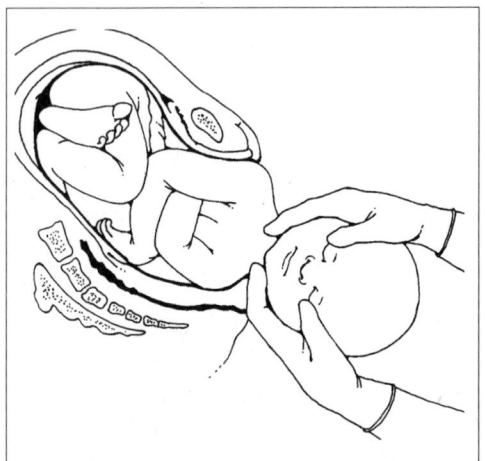

Don't pull on the baby. When the next contractions begins and mom bears down, gently guide the head in a downward motion to allow the anterior shoulder to deliver.

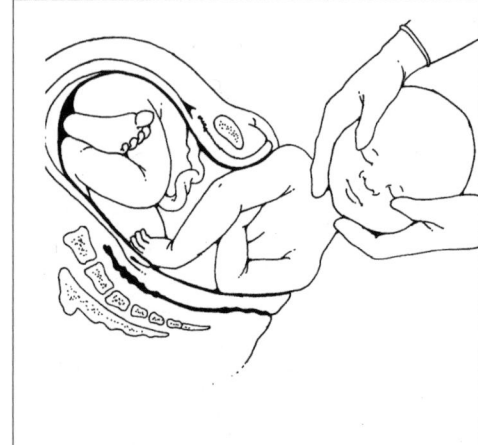

After the anterior shoulder delivers, guide the head upward gently to allow the rest of the body to be born.

118

- **Support the head as it emerges.** When the head is out, **run your fingers around the baby's neck to check for loops of cord.** Pull the loops over his head to dislodge them so he can breathe.

- When the head is born, **wipe the mucus from his nose and mouth.**

- **Don't pull on the baby.** There's no hurry. After the head delivers, the baby sits there until the next contraction when mom bears down; the shoulders will rotate on their own, and then the body will follow easily. When she bears down, you can gently guide the head in a downward motion to allow the anterior shoulder to deliver, then guide the head upward gently to allow the rest of the body to be born.

- **Dry him thoroughly** before wrapping him in a blanket. He'll become distressed if he's wet and gets too cold.

- **Wrap your baby in a warm towel or blanket.** Cover her head with a blanket or hat. Babies lose heat through the tops of their heads.

- **Put him to breast** to help the uterus contract and prevent excess bleeding.

- If you **keep his head a little lower than his body**, any excess secretions can drain out more easily.

- **Do Not Cut the Cord** or pull on it. The placenta will deliver on its own in about 15 minutes or less. It's a closed system between the baby and the placenta, so it's safer to wait until the doctor can take care of it. Wrap the placenta with the baby after it delivers.

- After the placenta delivers, **place your hand on your wife's abdomen and locate the uterus.** It feels like a firm grapefruit. Massage it every few minutes to keep it firm.

- Proceed to the hospital.

ΔΔΔ

13

LABOR AND BIRTH

PRE-BOUT JITTERS

Your wife announces that the time has come. She thinks her contractions are for real. Your swelling wave of excitement dashes on the shore of creeping panic. Your mind shifts into replay, hastily reviewing the strategies for your personal heavyweight bout with labor. You feel like you have a lot to remember, and it's normal to experience performance anxiety. You wonder if anyone really does all those exercises you learned in class, if they work, and if you'll remember what to do.

> **"I'm excited and looking forward to it, but I'm concerned if I will remember the breathing techniques and how to recognize real labor when it happens. I also worry about being at home when she needs me."**

THE WARM-UP

Labor is precisely what the term implies. For all but the lucky few, the work is hard and takes time. There are three phases to the labor process. The early phase is the warm-up. The contractions at this time shorten and thin the cervix. This process occurs before any significant dilatation can begin.

It's important to remind your wife that the main event hasn't begun yet. At this stage her contractions will be irregular, bouncing anywhere from 5 to 20 minutes apart, and mild to moderate in intensity. She may still be smiling and talking through them. It isn't time to go to the hospital yet. She needs to continue her regular activities until active labor begins. It's too soon at this stage to use breathing exercises; it would be like going 10 rounds before the actual match: she would just exhaust herself. Have her drink fluids and eat light soups, such as chicken noodle. She needs to keep up her strength, but she has to curb her cravings for chilidogs and burgers. It's common to vomit during the transition stage of labor.

> **"My wife had a lot of false labor for about 3 days, so we were both getting exasperated."**
>
> **"We had been up for 4 nights straight with false labor, so by the time labor really started we were both exhausted. I felt like I was in the Twilight Zone."**

THE MAIN EVENT—TRUE LABOR
Signs and Symptoms

Most couples worry about knowing when it's the real thing so they don't go to the hospital too soon. Here's an easy way to evaluate the contractions.

Since everyone's pain tolerance is different, your fingertips are more objective about the quality of her contractions than your wife is. When she tells you she's starting a contraction, place your fingertips at the top of her abdomen. The uterine muscle contracts first at the top and moves downward to push the baby's head against the cervix. Your wife feels the pain in the lower segment of the uterus. Press your fingertips gently on top of her abdomen to feel how firm it is.

Mild Contractions. These contractions aren't too uncomfortable. To your fingertips, the abdomen feels as firm as the tip of your nose. You feel something there, but you can still make a dent in your wife's abdomen.

Moderate Contractions. These contractions make her stop what she's doing and pay attention, but they're not too bad. To your fingers they feel as firm as your chin. It's firmer than your nose, but you can still push in her abdomen.

Strong Contractions. We call these the toe curlers. She won't be smiling or talking through these contractions. Her abdomen is so tight and firm that you can't make a dent in it. It feels as firm as your forehead.

How Long? Start counting the seconds when her abdomen is tight, not when she starts to feel it in her back. You can only count the time the uterus is actually pushing the baby's head against the cervix. Stop counting when it starts to relax, not when it's completely gone. Most contractions last between 40 to 60 seconds.

How Far Apart? You count from the beginning of one contraction to the beginning of the next one as the time between contractions.

If this is your first baby, you can call her doctor to say you're going to the hospital when she has had moderate contractions every 5 minutes for one hour. If this isn't your first baby, you can usually wait until her contractions are 10 to 15 minutes apart before calling the doctor. You'll have the answers to the three questions: How long; how strong; and how far apart? If her water bag breaks, call her doctor regardless of whether or not she's having contractions.

You're assured that the main event has begun when the cervix is at least 3 centimeters dilated and the contractions are regular and moderate to firm in intensity. This is the start of the active stage of labor. Your wife's smile has disappeared, and she's concentrating very hard during the contractions. She can start using some of the breathing exercises now if she wishes. Labor with a first baby averages 12 to18 hours once "true" labor is established.

> **"I was so worried about her. She had no choice; she couldn't change her mind. I would have done it for her if I could."**

The Labor Bag
Your Supplies
- Chapstick or unscented lip balm
- Unscented lotion and powder or cornstarch for backrubs
- Socks for her cold feet
- List of phone numbers and change for phone
- Camera with several roles of film and fresh batteries for flash
- Tape recorder with batteries and tapes

- Her focal point
- Pillow
- Lollipops for when her mouth gets dry
- Snacks for you

Her Suitcase
- 2 or 3 short nightgowns, with front opening if she'll be nursing
- Bathrobe
- Slippers
- Underwear
- Nursing bras 2 to 3 if breast-feeding
- Toothbrush and toothpaste
- Shampoo, conditioner, brush, and comb
- $5 for miscellaneous items
- Address book, announcements, stationary, stamps
- Loose clothes to wear home

Baby Things
- 2 receiving blankets
- Outfit to wear home
- Pacifier if you're going to use one
- Infant car seat

You arrive at the hospital and you're as anxious as a long-tailed cat in a room full of rocking chairs. You start looking for a safe place to park yourself. In spite of its "homey" atmosphere, you're acutely aware this is still a hospital. You know you're supposed to be a part of the "team," but your confidence level is falling faster than an unopened parachute. This is a good time to stake out your territory and get to work. Introduce yourself to the nurse and remember her name; she's your backup. Your job is to support your wife. The nurse's job is to support you both in your efforts. She's in your corner. Your place is next to your wife, where you can provide coaching and encouragement. She'll need lots of both. Use the labor guide in this chapter to remind you of what to do when.

> **"I feel great about being present for birth, but also very anxious."**

JUST SAY YES

Anxiety and tension are the biggest enemies in labor. They have a negative effect on contractions. In an anxious mom, contractions may be frequent but not effective enough to promote normal progress in labor, which is considered approximately 1 centimeter per hour. If your wife is unable to relax with just the breathing exercises, or if she feels like she's losing control, a little medication can really help.

Pain relievers such as Demerol can be used in small amounts to take the edge off the pain. Very few women make it through labor without a little medication to help them tolerate and cope with the contractions. The baby is not depressed by the much smaller doses of medication. In between contractions, she can relax, which helps her conserve energy. Keep in mind that you're her advocate. During labor, women are usually more submissive and definitely vulnerable. She'll be looking to you for help and guidance in making decisions. If she's having a tough time, don't discourage her from requesting pain medication, or worse, tell her she can't have any.

WHAT A RELIEF

Regional anesthesia can be given during labor to numb the lower part of the abdomen to relieve pain from contractions and cervical dilatation. The most widely used regional anesthesia is the epidural. A novocaine-like drug is injected into a soft, plastic tube placed into the woman's back. The tube does not enter the spinal canal, and the headaches associated with a spinal block aren't usually a problem with epidurals. Potential side effects include a drop in maternal blood pressure, but this is usually avoided with intravenous fluids and ensuring that the woman doesn't lie on her back.

An epidural is usually given in the midpart of the active phase of labor and can be used right through delivery. The ideal epidural relieves pain but doesn't affect ability to move. The woman is better able to push and less likely to need forceps for the delivery. She's awake, alert, and comfortable. This is a particularly welcome form of pain relief for a first baby.

The timing for an epidural can be a little trickier with subsequent babies because labor progresses more rapidly. If your wife thinks she's interested in this type of anesthesia, put in your request before labor so the arrangements can be made if your hospital doesn't have 24-hour anesthesia coverage. More hospitals are now offering epidural anesthesia as an option during labor. Talk to your wife's doctor about any questions or concerns you have.

FETAL MONITORING

The fetal monitor is used to evaluate the relationship between the contractions and the fetal heart rate. For the baby, the process of labor is akin to running a marathon. Most babies are in good shape and can withstand the stress of intermittent decreases in oxygen. For the baby who doesn't have good reserves, labor can mean the difference between normal stress and distress.

Continuous fetal monitoring is usually reserved for those complications and situations where the baby may be at risk for distress, such as:

- Preeclampsia (pregnancy-induced hypertension)
- Diabetes
- Chronic hypertension
- Postdates pregnancy (42 plus weeks)
- Preterm labor (less than 37 weeks)
- Breech presentation
- Bleeding
- Meconium-stained amniotic fluid

For the mother low-risk mother, a 10 to 20 minute baseline recording may be done on admission and then repeated only once an hour.

The use of the fetal monitor shouldn't interfere with an intimate birth experience. Your wife doesn't need to be confined to bed; she can still sit in a chair or stand by the bedside.

Nursing personnel should fully explain how the monitor works and why it's being used and provide ongoing reports of how well your baby is tolerating the contractions. Keep in mind that the fetal monitor cannot prevent or detect neurological problems (brain damage); it only tells us if the baby is currently receiving enough oxygen for the central nervous system to function normally. A normal tracing is 99 percent predictive of a good outcome.

Monitoring Methods

The two methods of fetal monitoring are external and internal. The external method is easy to use. Two belts are strapped around your wife's abdomen. One device records the frequency and duration of contractions; the other one records the fetal heart rate. The two disadvantages of this method are the discomfort from the belts and the difficulty in maintaining a good recording of the fetal heart rate. If the baby moves out of the range of the ultrasound beam, the recording pen either stops or jumps all over the paper. It can be panic time if you think your baby's heart has stopped. Just call the nurse, and she'll come and readjust the belts and everything will look normal again.

The internal method is more comfortable since the belts are eliminated. Frequently, a combination of the internal electrode to directly record the baby's heart rate and the external belt to record contractions are used during labor. Only an internal catheter will evaluate accurately the strength of the uterine contractions. If your wife seems to be having adequate contractions but she isn't progressing in labor, her doctor may want to use the catheter before deciding to start oxytocin to stimulate stronger contractions.

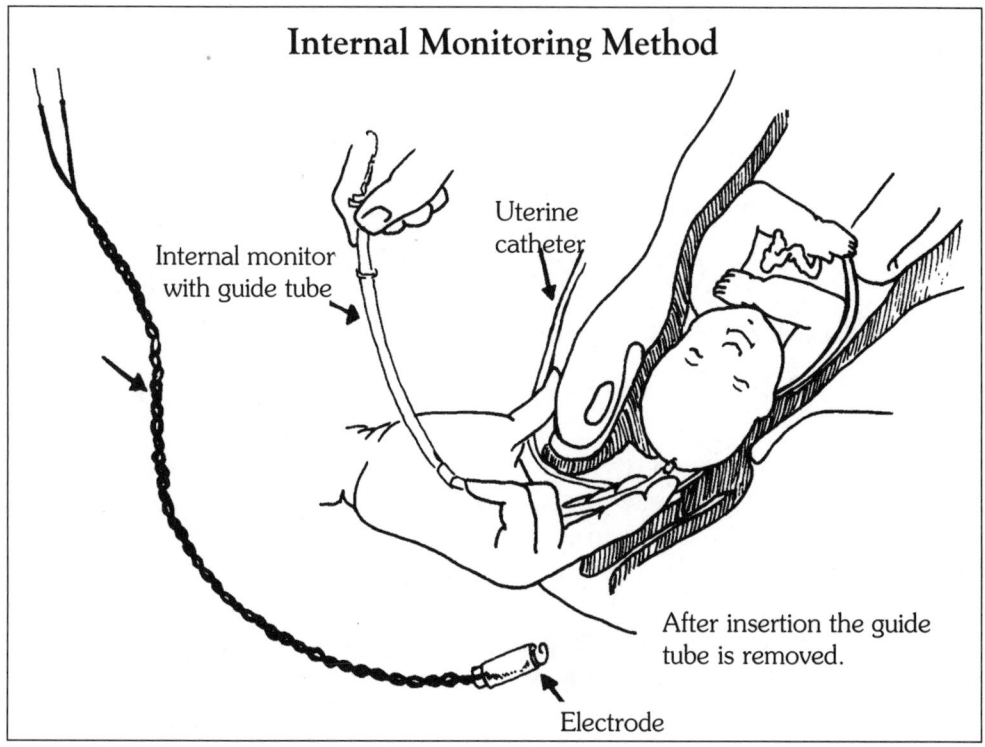

Internal Monitoring Method

Internal monitor with guide tube

Uterine catheter

After insertion the guide tube is removed.

Electrode

Breathless

Four deceleration patterns are seen during labor, with variable decelerations being the most common. Variables usually occur when the the baby and the umbilical cord are squeezed during contractions. On the monitor strip, the heart rate takes an abrupt nose dive from 120 to 160 beats per minute to sometimes 60 beats per minute. This pattern can be very distressing if you don't understand what's happening. It looks terrifying, but it isn't for the baby. The sequence is similar to taking a big deep breath and then holding it for 40 to 50 seconds. You let the air out and rest for 10 to 15 seconds and then take another big breath. You can repeat this sequence for long periods of time without any distress. It works the same way for your baby. Most babies tolerate variable decelerations quite well, even when they go as low as 60 beats per minute. It's reassuring when the heart rate jumps right back up to a normal heart rate after the contraction lets up. As soon as the cord is no longer being squeezed by the contractions, the baby quickly reoxygenates and gets ready for the next contractions.

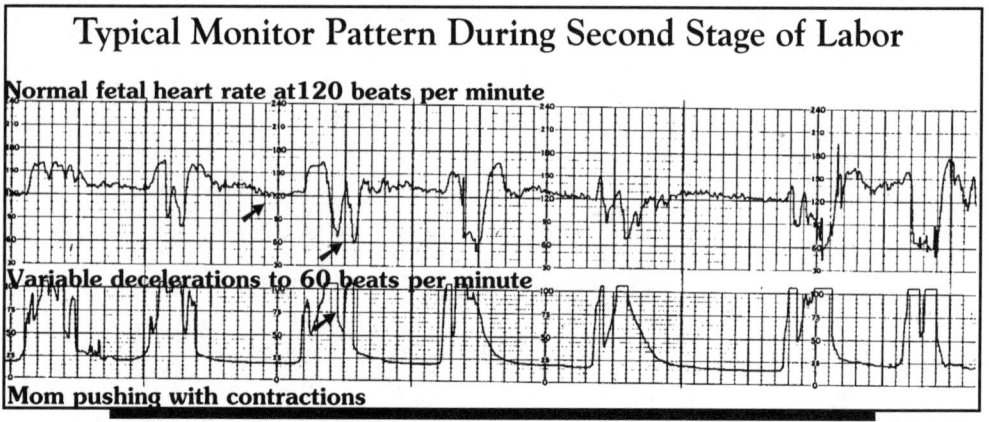

COMFORTING THE COACH

Labor is stressful for you too. Prepared childbirth classes help but can't totally allay your own fears and anxiety. You have to deal with your own feelings as you watch your wife in pain. Involving yourself in your role of coach will keep you busy and help you keep your perspective.

> **"It was hard watching my wife in pain. She was given an epidural but it only took on one side so she didn't get much relief."**

Don't forget to be good to yourself. Periodically, you may need a break after hours of coaching. Ask the labor nurse, or other support person, to give you a break; she or he can stay with her while you take a breather. Try some relaxation techniques on yourself and eat something. Consider bringing snacks of fruit, trailmix, and peanut butter sandwiches, which work better than candy bars to keep your blood sugar even. If your blood sugar is low, you can become exhausted and frazzled and your wife will sense it. Your calm confidence can be conveyed to her through your sense of well-being and soothing touch. Consider having a support person present for *you*, someone who's optimistic, upbeat, and understanding to cheer you on.

> **"The nurses were wonderful. They seemed to know when I needed a break and would come in and tell me to go take a walk in some fresh air. I guess they could see I was overwhelmed."**

PREFERRED POSITIONS

Different positions in labor produce different results in the quality and quantity of contractions. The quality of contractions is more important than the quantity. Force dilates the cervix. Strong contractions 3 to 4 minutes apart are preferable to 2-minute contractions that are only moderate in intensity. The uterus is a muscle and needs sufficient time between contractions to reoxygenate. If contractions are closer than 3 minutes, they aren't as effective.

Discourage your wife from lying on her back, especially flat on her back, because this position can cut off the blood supply to her and the baby. Her blood pressure can drop dangerously and cut off the baby's oxygen supply. Contractions

129

are also more frequent but less intense in this position. Lying on her side or sitting in a chair promote stronger contractions that are further apart and more effective in dilating the cervix. You don't want to spend any more time with the labor process than necessary.

CHEERS

During the active phase of labor, as your wife's concentration becomes more intense, you may feel as if you aren't really needed. Be assured—you are. She just isn't interested in small talk. She won't be able to cope with anything but limited conversation and direction. Keep your sentences brief and use positive words for direction. For instance, say "Relax" instead of "Don't tense up"; "Blow" rather than "Don't push." Remember to use that soft hypnotic voice that will transform her to her relaxing place.

> **"It took us a while to get into a good pattern of working together with the breathing patterns, but after a few hours, we felt like pros."**

If others are present, check with your wife periodically to see if she's still comfortable with more than just you in the labor room. She may decide that she can't cope with too big an audience. You can run interference for her and send everyone out for snacks. If you find yourself in the situation where she isn't progressing, that may be a signal that she needs some time away from the support group. She can get performance anxiety, which affects her labor.

ROUND 8

The most difficult time in labor is the transition phase. At this time the cervix is about 8 centimeters dilated and the end is near. The contractions are now incredibly intense. Keep your voice soft and your head cool if she flies off the handle with some undeleted expletives. Even the most fragile flower of womanhood has been known to temporarily use vocabulary that would make a truck driver blush— much to her husband's horror. Don't worry. The nurses have heard it all before. Luckily, this period is very short. Hang in there with her. Keep reminding her it is almost over.

ROUND 10

By this time the cervix is fully dilated. Both of you are feeling euphoric. The pain from dilating the cervix has been replaced by the urge to push as the baby moves down the birth canal. The end is almost in sight. You become ecstatically encouraged as you begin to see a small patch of hair peeking out as your wife pushes. First babies don't usually fall out. It isn't unusual to push for an hour before the baby is born (subsequent babies come faster).

You can help keep your wife calm by ensuring that only one person at a time is providing verbal direction. Too much input can be confusing and distracting to her, especially during this second stage when she's pushing. When you have a lot of support people, they can get excited with everyone trying to cheer her on at the same time. Explain to them that she can pay attention to only one voice. Your voice is her anchor in the stormy sea of intense physical sensations that she is experiencing. She needs to be able to focus her attention to follow your directions.

> **"She told me if she hadn't had my voice to hang onto for guidance, she didn't think she could have made it through delivery."**

EPISIOTOMY

As the baby's head shows more and more with each push, the doctor will have to decide whether or not to do an episiotomy. It's impossible to tell in advance if one is needed because there are too many variables to consider, such as the size of the baby's head in relation to the ability of the tissues to stretch. Even if an episiotomy isn't done, it still doesn't guarantee that there won't be any stitches. With a first baby, pushing can take an hour, or sometimes more. If your wife becomes too tired to push, she might welcome some help to speed things along. If it looks like she might tear, an episiotomy would be done in most cases. Most doctors prefer repairing a smooth incision to a ragged tear.

The episiotomy process may seen a little gruesome to most men. The automatic reaction is to cross your legs even thinking about it. In actuality, it isn't painful, even if performed without anesthesia, as long as the baby's head is crowning well. The tissue becomes very thin and the pressure of the baby's head

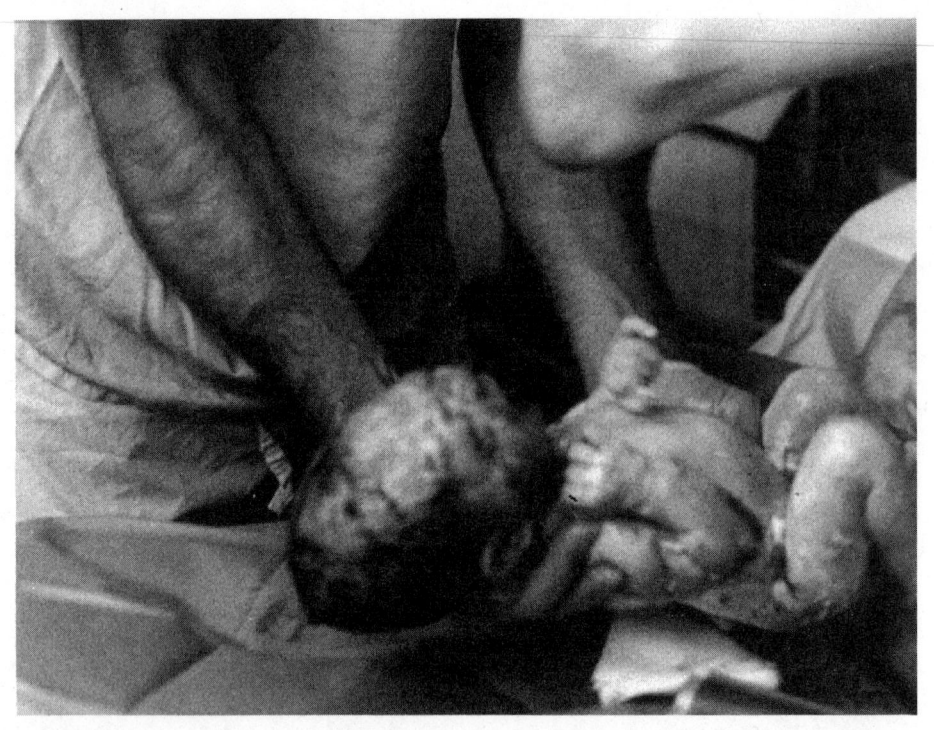

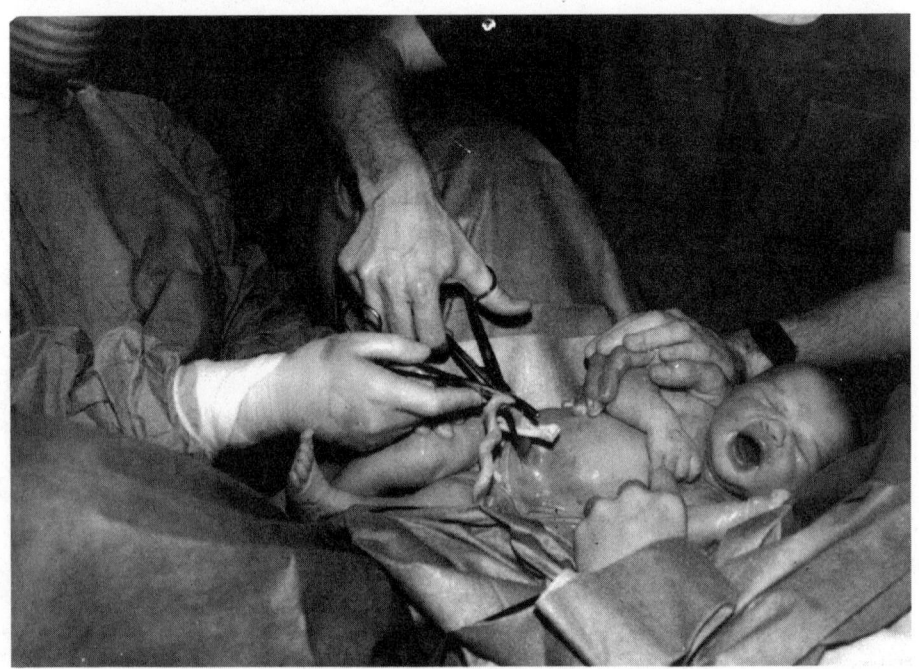

anesthetizes the nerves in the area. As a rule, a novocaine-like drug is injected to ensure that the area is numb before the incision is made. It isn't mandatory for you to watch the episiotomy being performed, especially if you feel squeamish.

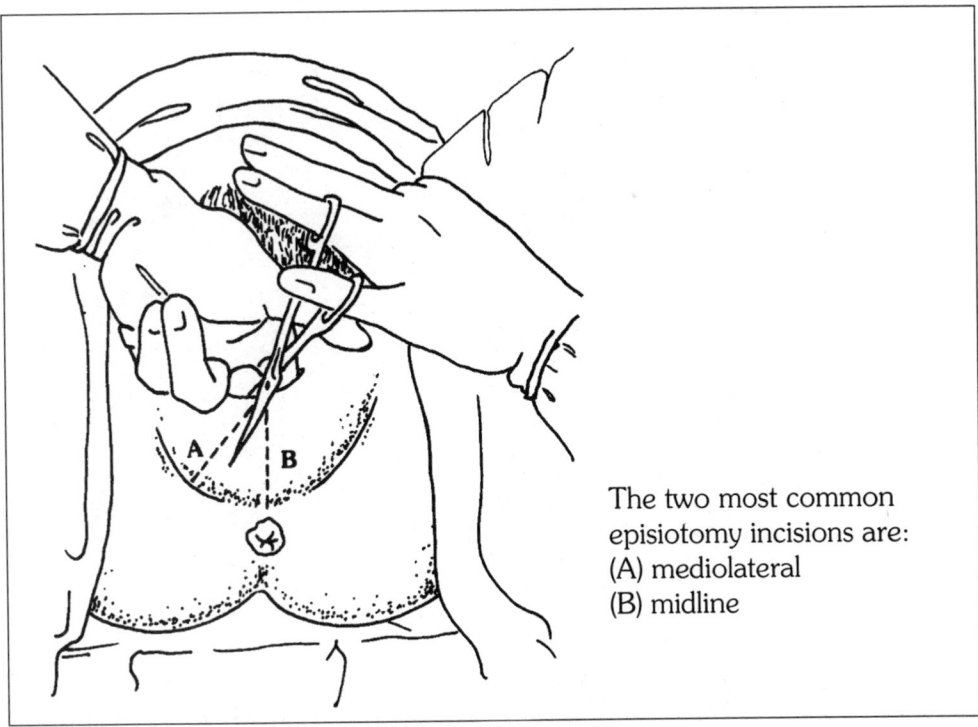

The two most common episiotomy incisions are:
(A) mediolateral
(B) midline

The most common episiotomy is the midline, which heals quickly and leaves a minimum of discomfort. The stitches dissolve in 10 to 14 days. Most women who have had a midline episiotomy agree that it's not a big deal. Encourage your wife to be flexible. This is one of those times you have to trust your doctor's judgment and experience.

MAGIC MOMENTS

The moment you have spent many anxious months waiting for has just happened. Your baby is actually here! Be prepared. Real newborns do not look like babies on the front of food jars. Newborns in the first minutes after birth are more dusky blue than pretty pink. Their cardiovascular systems have to make the switch from inside to outside wiring. As the blood becomes oxygenated from breathing and crying, they become more pink. The hands and feet stay blue the longest.

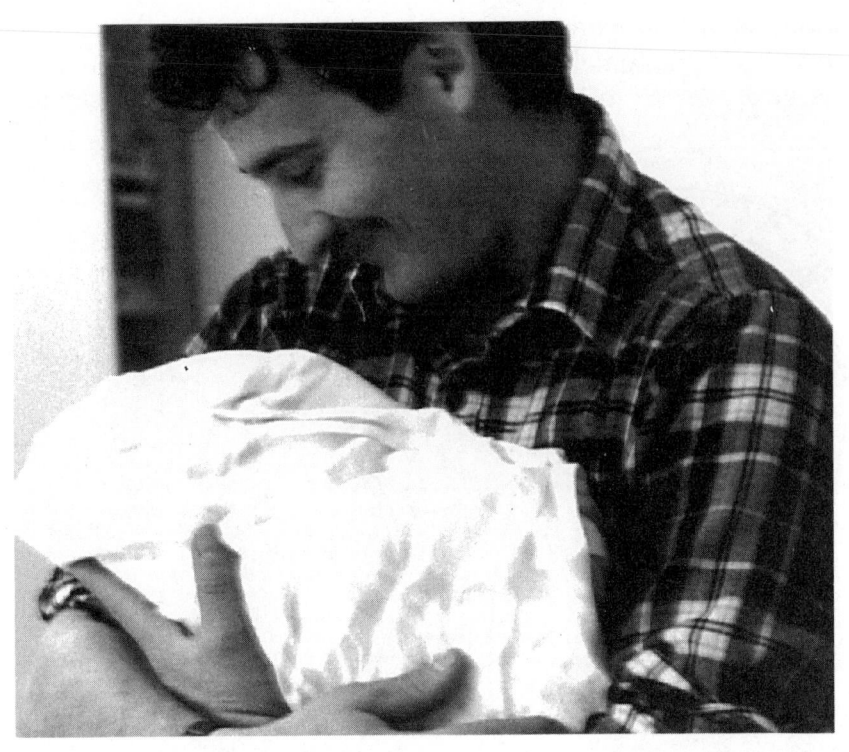

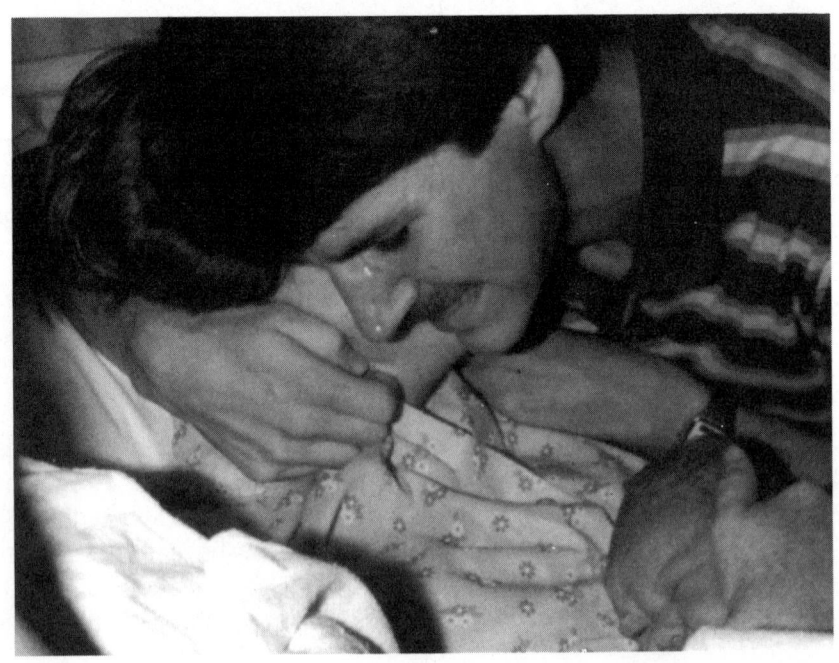

Newborns are also very messy. They're covered with blood from the placenta and vernix is still slathered all over the body. Most nurses wipe off the worst of the mess before wrapping the baby snugly in the blanket for you to hold.

Most newborns have heads that seem misshapen. It can be a little disconcerting if you don't know what to expect. The head is very malleable as it inches down the birth canal and assumes whatever shape makes the trip easier. Not to worry. By the time you take your baby home, her head will have molded to a more attractive and normal shape.

You hold her and you can't take your eyes off her. You begin to appreciate the miracle you've helped conceive as you take inventory and examine all her fingers, toes, and the other standard parts. You run the tips of your fingers over her face and you hold her close. Your feelings of relief, love, and protectiveness can be pretty intense. You might even shed a tear or two. Don't be bashful. The hospital staff thinks its touching too. No matter how many times they see a baby being born, the reaction is the same: euphoria and wonder.

> **"Once that beautiful baby's head came out, I started to cry. I had never felt anything like that before."**
>
> **"I felt like I had run a marathon by the time she was born. I have never been that drained before."**

APGAR SCORE

At 1 and 5 minutes after birth, your baby's heart rate, muscle tone, color, respirations, and cry will be evaluated according to the Apgar scoring system, a

APGAR SCORE

SIGN	0	1	2
Heart rate	Absent	Slow—below 100	Above 100
Respiratory effort	Absent	Slow—irregular	Good crying
Muscle tone	Flaccid	Some flexion of extremities	Active motion
Reflex irritability	None	Grimace	Vigorous cry
Color	Pale blue	Body pink—blue extremities	Completely pink
		TOTAL	9

simple preliminary test of his heart and lung function as he adapts to the outside world. It's not an IQ test or a long-range predictor of health. Points are given for each category. A score of 7 to 10 indicates that the heart and lungs are doing their job. For all you over-achievers, very few babies get a 10 in the first minute, so don't start lobbying for a higher score.

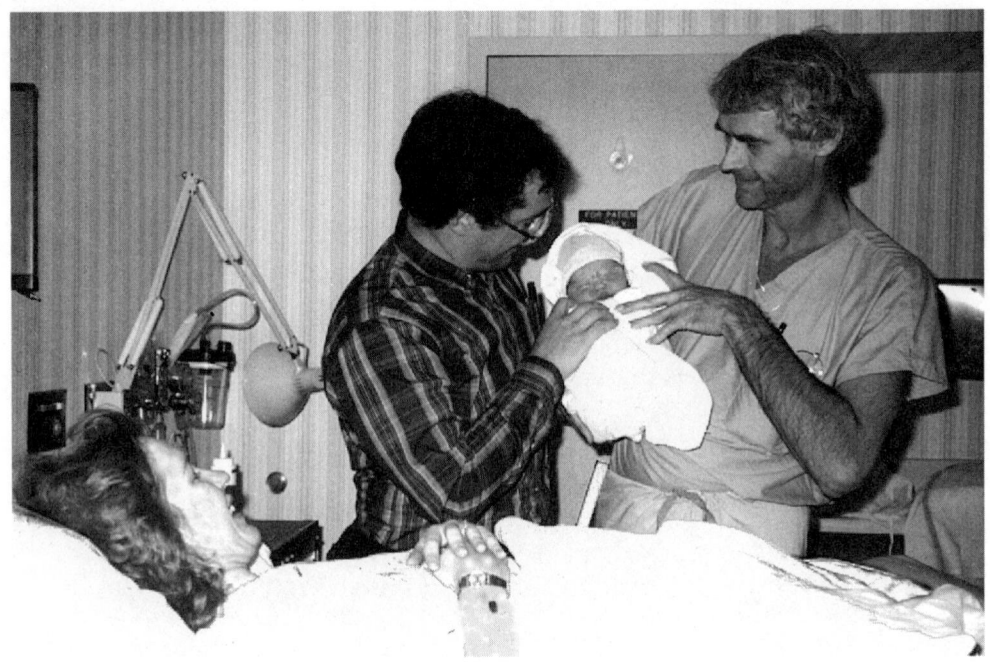

EYE DROPS

All newborns have their eyes treated with antibiotic ointment to prevent possible infection from gonorrhea. In times past, silver nitrate was used, which was very irritating to the newborns' eyes. Unlike silver nitrate, the antibiotic ointment doesn't cause puffiness and swelling.

CESAREAN BIRTH

It doesn't hurt to give some thought to which type of anesthesia your wife would prefer—general or epidural—if a cesarean birth is necessary. Epidural anesthesia is very popular because the mother can be awake and be part of the experience. Most hospitals now allow the father and even a support person to be present during the procedure and birth of their baby. Many hospitals do the cesarean in the obstetrical department, which is a homier atmosphere than a regular surgery suite.

If your wife has general anesthesia, it's still possible for you to be present for the birth of your baby. She may be asleep, but your new baby isn't. The two of you can get acquainted right away. If you would rather not be there during surgery, you can still see your baby right after. Be sure and fill your wife in on all the details she missed. It's an important process to help her bridge the gap between being pregnant and being a mother. She needs to know what time the baby was born, Apgar score, weight, length, and any other details you can remember.

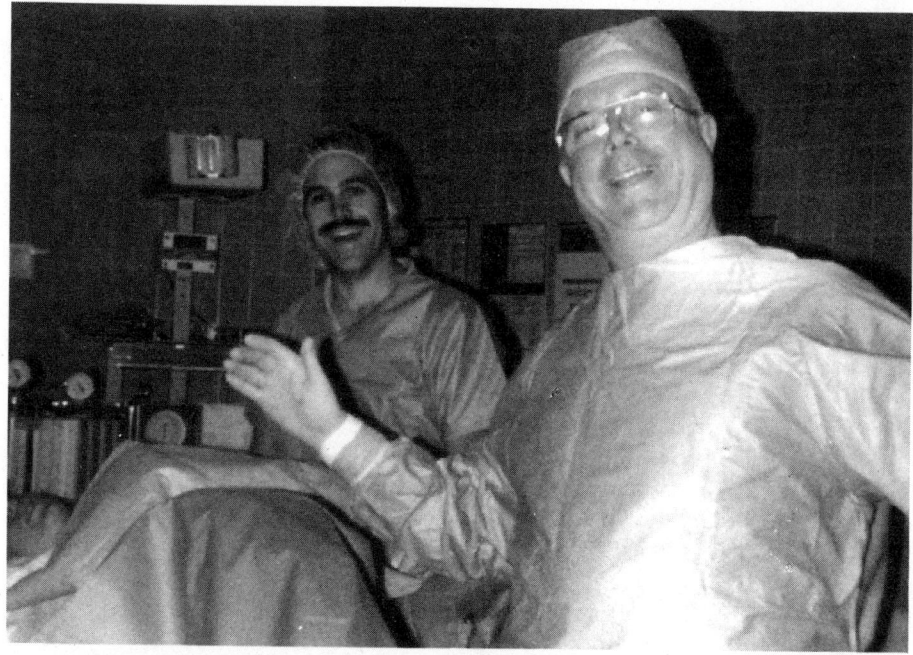

"I was so relieved when the doctor finally decided she needed a cesarean. She was in labor so long and wasn't getting anywhere, so I felt useless."

"I was a little disappointed, but glad it was going to be over soon."

An unplanned cesarean birth is very traumatic for most couples. Anxiety reaches an all-time high after hours of not progressing in labor or fetal distress develops. The mother is usually exhausted and demoralized. Her husband feels frantic and helpless. It's common for both to feel as if they have somehow failed.

> **"I felt very helpless. I had really prepared to play an active role during labor and delivery, but the baby was breech so I felt a little cheated."**

It's important to realize that you both go through a process of grieving for what should have been. You prepared for and expected a normal vaginal delivery, but it didn't happen that way. Shock sets in as preparations are made for the surgery. Relief comes after the birth, and then anger can take its place. Especially if things happen very quickly, there are always questions about what happened and why. What could you have done differently? Don't hesitate to discuss your feelings with each other and with her doctor. It's better to clear up any doubts or misunderstanding now, and her doctor will appreciate the opportunity to help you feel better about the circumstances.

> **"It was extremely difficult to be in the operating room. During our classes, I thought it would be easy to be there, but when reality hit, it was tough seeing that happen to someone I love."**
>
> **"We're ready to sign up for another one. Her surgery and recovery went so well."**

TIES THAT BIND—THE BONDING PROCESS

Most hospitals let your baby stay with you the first hour or so after birth so you can start the getting-acquainted process known as bonding. You and your wife may discover that the overwhelming love you thought would automatically captivate you didn't happen right away. Your feelings and attachment for your new baby evolve and grow, just as they did with your wife. It takes time.

Initially, you might even find your're disappointed if the sex of your real baby doesn't match your fantasy baby. You've been carrying a picture around in your head about how this new baby was going to look and be. Now you have to reconcile fantasy with reality. It doesn't mean that you aren't pleased and grateful for your new baby: you just have a little adjusting to do. Your wife goes through the same process. It's normal.

△△△

LABOR GUIDE

EARLY LABOR -- 1-3 CMS DILATION

Physical Changes	Emotional Changes	Activities and Support
Contractions mild, irregular, short duration (30-40 seconds).	Anxious, but excited	Drink fluids, eat lightly. Continue normal activities.
Cramps and low backache		Use relaxation exercises. Wait to start breathing exercises. Don't focus on contractions.
May have bloody show and mild diarrhea.		Have her visualize the cervix softening and becoming very thin.
		Call doctor when contractions every 10 min. for multip and every 5 min for primip.

ACTIVE LABOR -- 4-7 CMS DILATION

Physical Changes	Emotional Changes	Activities and Support
Contractions *every* 2-5 min. More intense. Lasting 50-60 seconds.	Anxious for progress	Change position often. Keep upright as long as possible.
Bloody show may increase.	Tendency to be tense	Visualize baby pushing on cervix; uterus working well; your calm peaceful place;everything working in harmony and flowing.
Water bag may break		
	Needs encouragement.	Praise her. Have doctor or nurse tell her how much progress she is making.

ACTIVE LABOR (CONT)

Physical Changes	Emotional Changes	Activities and Suport
	More withdrawn. Less talkative.	Speak softly. Keep sentences simple and brief.
	More difficult to remain calm and centered. Very irritable if disturbed during contractions.	Delay caretaking activities during contractions.
May hyperventilate.	Can feel panicky.	Encourage slow breathing. Rhythmically stroke her forehead to calm and distract her.
Pain with contractions.	May worry about being able to cope with contractions	Encourage breathing exercises through contractions Consider med-ication.
Pain in hips and thighs.		Massage feet at back of lower heel, the acupressure site for hip pain.
May need to urinate		Help her to bathroom every hour. Ask nurse to help.
Lips may become chapped.		Apply glycerine. Offer ice chips.
If progress slows or stops	May become discouraged	Walk. Discuss other options with nurse or doctor (oxytocin or medication).

TRANSITION 8-10 CMS DILATION

Physical Changes	Emotional Changes	Activities and Support
Contractions 1-2 min. apart. Lasting 60-90 seconds at their strongest	May become irrational and paranoid. Common to want medication.	Breathing exerice #3 to keep from pushing too soon.
May feel intense pressure in perineum and urge to push.	Can feel overwhelmed with physical sensations.	Use positive directions. Say "Blow," not, "Don't push." Remind her this stage is short.
		Try semi-sitting position to help baby move down.
Face is flushed.		Use cold cloth to face.
May become nauseated		Locate emesis basin
Leg cramp may strike.		Grasp toes and push ball of foot backward to stretch calf muscles. Hold positon until cramp relieved.

SECOND STAGE

Physical Changes	Emotional Changes	Activities and Support
Contractions stronger but she feels some relief from pain.	Exhausted and euphoric	Assume squatting or side-lying position.
Feels pressure and urge to pursh.	Finds energy to push.	Encourage her to push with urge.
Perineum bulges as baby's head descends. Crowning occurs when you see part of baby's head.	Peaceful and sleepy between contractions	Suggest she visualize the baby moving down with each push, her perineum relaxed and yielding. Think-calm and confident.

SUMMARY OF LABOR MEDICATIONS

Type -Name-Dose	Benefits	Precautions
Narcotics Demerol 25-50 mg IV every 2 hours 50-100 mg IM every 3-4 hours	Does not slow labor. Good pain relief Decreases anxiety; allows sleep between contractions	Nausea and vomiting if given too rapidly. Possible respiratory depression if given in large doses.
Stadol 1-2 mg IV or IM	Less respiratory depressant effect than other narcotics.	Cannot be given before Demerol. Makes it ineffective.
Morphine 2-3 mg IV 10-15 mg IM	Good pain relief No effect on labor Used to treat prolonged latent phase of labor.	Respiratory depression with high doses. Not routinely used for active labor. Effective for prolonged latent phase.
Nubain 10 mg IM or IV	Good pain relief Enhances relaxation in early labor	Can produce respiratory depression in baby.
Talwin Ketamine		Not recommended. Potential psychotic reaction and dream disturbance.
Anti-Anxiety Vistaril 50-100 mg IM 50-100 mg orally	Decreases anxiety	IM injection painful. Oral administration preferred.
Valium Sparine Phenergan Largon	None	Not recommended for labor. Causes depression in newborn
Sedatives Seconal Nembutal		Not recommended for labor.

14

BEYOND BIRTH

You're home with your wife and baby, and you're anxious to settle in and get back to normal—or what you remember of it.

THE EARLY DAZE

The first week or two can be very hectic. Your dream girl still isn't back to normal. Her behavior makes you feel like you've been zapped back into the twilight zone of the first trimester: she's tired, tearful, and very testy. Her euphoria during the first few days after giving birth has waned. It's normal to experience a letdown after the intense high of giving birth. She's left with all-out fatigue, and she looks and acts like the bride of Dracula—pale and pooped. She probably feels unloved, unlovable, and unattractive. She may not be as thrilled about the baby as she was in the hospital. He may be spending more time in his crib, but don't worry; she hasn't changed her mind about being a mother. When she overcomes her fatigue and he becomes more charming, she'll start spending more time with him. She just has a lot to cope with both emotionally and physically right now.

> **"Our first night home was traumatic. We had been pampered so much in the hospital; it was an unsettling feeling knowing that now it was all up to us."**

Emotional upsets are common the first 10 days. They're often referred to as the "baby blues." The most common reason for the baby blues is the raging sleep deficit most women experience during those first months after birth. Lack of sleep can make anyone crazy. Keep this in mind when your wife seems a little incoherent and disoriented at times in those first few weeks. If the upsets are still around by the end of the first 2 weeks, she needs to talk to her doctor to make sure she isn't experiencing a real depression. Few women experience a real postpartum depression and need professional help, but it doesn't hurt to check it out. You also need to reevaluate how much help you're providing. She may be trying to do too much, which contributes to her fatigue and baby blues. Now's the time to rack up some very important brownie points. Decide in advance which caretaking duties you're willing and able to manage. If you can, reach an agreement before the birth, when she's calm, coherent, and rational. If you don't clearly commu-

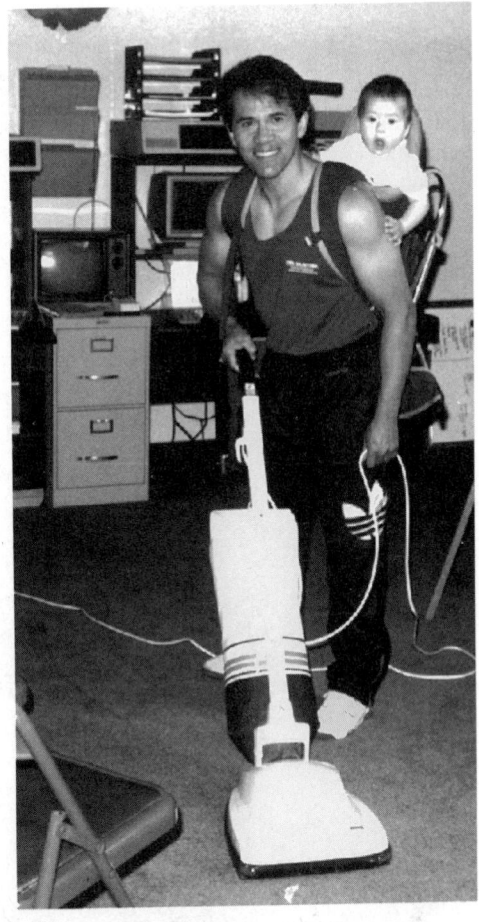

nicate your mutual expectations, you can sow seeds of discontent that produce unwanted weeds in your garden of love later. Your helpfulness, patience, and stable influence will reap major benefits. As the old song pointed out, "*Little Things Mean A Lot.*" Watch the baby while she naps. Take the phone off the hook so she won't be disturbed. Send out for Chinese food. Help with the night feedings and housework. She won't forget you were there for her when she needed you. It's a most worthwhile investment.

> **"My wife had a very difficult 2 weeks with the baby blues. I found myself getting depressed too. The two of us would sit there together at 2 A.M. and cry for the next 2 hours. It was awful."**

Physically your wife experiences a myriad of aches and pains left over from pregnancy and birth while her body is trying to get back to normal. She's in a mopey funk because she still looks about 4 months pregnant. She may be back to her prepregnant weight, but several crucial pounds have shifted like the sands of the Sahara and made lumps in conspicuous places she isn't happy about. Remind her that few women manage to regain their movie goddess figure right away; many are distressed by the pounds that persevere a year later, but she doesn't need to hear that right now. Reassure her that you think she's still beautiful. Let her know you love her and that you're confident those extra pounds and mounds will melt with time, a sensible diet, and exercise.

> **"Things are starting to settle down a little now. It looks as though there might be life after birth."**

FATHERLY FEELINGS

You never thought you would ever gush over a baby, but here you are spewing over like Old Faithful whenever you look at her. You want to talk about her to anyone who'll listen. You and your wife look for family resemblances. She has your eyes and Uncle Dave's dimpled chin. You're still in the binding-bonding process that began at birth and will continue over the next 6 months or so.

> **"I never thought I would have those feelings of falling in love again, but when I saw that baby's head come out and she stretched her arm out, my heart melted."**
>
> **"We are starting to relax a little, but I am still pretty over protective with him.'**

Hand in hand with those intense feelings of love, wonder, and protectiveness for your new baby can be disconcerting feelings of jealousy and insecurity. Your wife doesn't have as much time to "baby" you now that she has a real one. If she's breast-feeding, you can resent the baby using and enjoying what used to be your exclusive property. You can have all the talks you want with yourself about how only a jerk would feel that way, but it's important to recognize that those feelings are normal. Don't be hard on yourself; it's part of that psychological shift from couple

to family. The first few weeks at home are stressful for you too. The focus is on your wife, but you need a few kind words and some support. Remember that the crisis is temporary. You're both doing a lot of psychological and physical shifting to make room for your expanded family. Let her know how you're feeling so she can reciprocate the reassurance and support you've been giving her; it's a two-way street.

> "I wasn't prepared for the intensity of the bonding that goes on. My life is so totally wrapped up in this little bundle."

> "The best part of becoming a father was the realization that I was capable of such total selfless love."

MACHO MAN OR MR. MOM?

Fathering is not a spectator sport. Until now, in the parenting game, you've been warming the bench. Now you've been promoted to first string. You wonder if you can measure up to your idea of what an ideal father should be.

In the last few years, the concept of "fathering" has done an about-face. Society's values and expectations have changed. But what do you do? If real men don't eat quiche, do they change diapers and feed babies? Absolutely!!!

Most men initially feel insecure about being a father, particularly about the caretaking role. Men who think nothing of fearlessly running down a football field with a herd of giants hot on their trail can be easily intimidated by a tiny bundle of joy. Things are more simple than you think. For example, you hold a football and a baby the same way, and it's a lot less hazardous. You've had a lot more experience than you thought. You feel all thumbs just looking at a diaper? Not to worry. You can hone your manual skills before your baby is born. Community classes offer baby care. You can easily learn feeding, bathing, diapering, and infant massage if you need help.

The freeway to fatherhood can be a little bumpy, but the trip can be made smoother if you take an active role in caring for your baby with feeding, cuddling, and diaper changing. To build a solid foundation in any relationship, you have to spend time together and get to know each other. It's the same with you and your baby. Buy a baby carrier and take walks together. Practice those new communication skills you learned. Make a weekend routine of giving him a massage. Borrow the rocking chair, snuggle up, and talk to him often. Start living that mental image you have of what a daddy should be. The more you become involved in caring for your baby, the more confident you become—and the more you enjoy being a dad.

> **"I was not prepared for the overwhelming responsibility."**
>
> **"I could never understand parents when they talked about giving up their life for their kids, but I sure do now."**

After about a month, you'll both be ready to breakaway and go somewhere alone—anywhere! She wants out. Oblige her—take her to dinner, dancing, or a movie. Don't be surprised if you find you're both spending all your time talking about the baby. Halfway through the evening you may decide to go home because you feel guilty and miss her. You've passed another milestone in the bonding process.

GETTING TO KNOW YOU

Most couples, the first time around, are very apprehensive about how they're going to know what their baby needs and when. It's very confusing trying to decode what each little noise and cry means. It won't take long before you get the hang of it. You learn to recognize the hungry cry from the fussy "I want some attention" cry or the "I'm too tired to do anything else" cry. It's common sense, intuition, and paying attention.

> **"Rarely does anyone tell you that all they do is sleep, eat, and cry for the first months."**

Each baby comes equipped with a unique temperament ready for expression from the first breath. Ask any delivery room nurse. Some babies are as mellow as a marathoner at the finish line. "No sweat" is their motto from the first hour. Others arrive into the world as anxious as an actor without an audience. They need a lot of attention, comforting, and reassuring to alleviate their anxiety.

We all know that babies cry when they're hungry, but they cry for other reasons too Sometimes they cry as a way to relieve tension. Babies cry when they're tired or

overstimulated. Many babies have a certain time of the day when they're routinely fussy. They can't jog, meditate, or work out, so they cry. One fourth of all newborns have crying periods 3 times a week that last 3 or more hours. You can set your clock by them. The dinner hour is a popular time with many babies.

Some babies are able to console themselves quite well. One might cry for a few minutes, stick a fist in his mouth, and drop off to sleep. Other babies can be inconsolable no matter what you do. Try not take it personally if your baby falls into the inconsolable category. Consider it a challenge to figure out what soothes his soul, and eventually you'll figure it out. Here are some tips to remember for those fussy times.

COMFORTING WAYS

- *Swaddling* your baby is a wonderful old Indian custom of wrapping the baby tightly in a blanket with his arms inside. Restricting movement seems to be calming. Kind of like the old days in the womb—warm and confining.

- *The plug* can be a thumb, fist or pacifier. Some babies have a greater need to suck than others. If a pacifier makes him happy, do it.

- *Temperature* changes can sometimes disturb your baby. Check to see if you have too many or too few clothes on her. Judge by how you're dressed. If you have two layers of clothes on and she has six, she's probably too warm.

- *Sounds* can be soothing. Devices that mimic the sound of the placenta, ocean waves, or a heartbeat can be comforting. Tape your baby's own crying and play it back to him, sometimes has a quieting effect. Play soothing music. For the really hard to console baby, try a car ride, or put your baby in a seat on top of the dryer while it's running, but don't leave her alone. They like the motion.

- *Rocking chairs and swings* work well. Get a long windup time for the swing. They're great for dinner times, when your wife is tired of eating with one hand while you cut up her meat.

- *Baby carriers* work well for babies who like constant contact. The ones that strap to your front also allow the baby to hear your heartbeat.

If you've tried the entire repertoire and nothing works, accept what you can't change for now. Put Sweetness in her crib on her stomach and get out your ear plugs. You've done all you can.

SUPPING AND SLEEPING

The first 4 weeks, your baby will want to be fed every 3 to 4 hours—through the night. If she's being bottle-fed, you can split the night shift and share the sleep deficit. If your wife is breast-feeding, you can still help by getting up at night at least half the time to bring the baby to her in bed so she doesn't have to get up. You can change her and put her back to bed so your wife can get back to her much needed sleep.

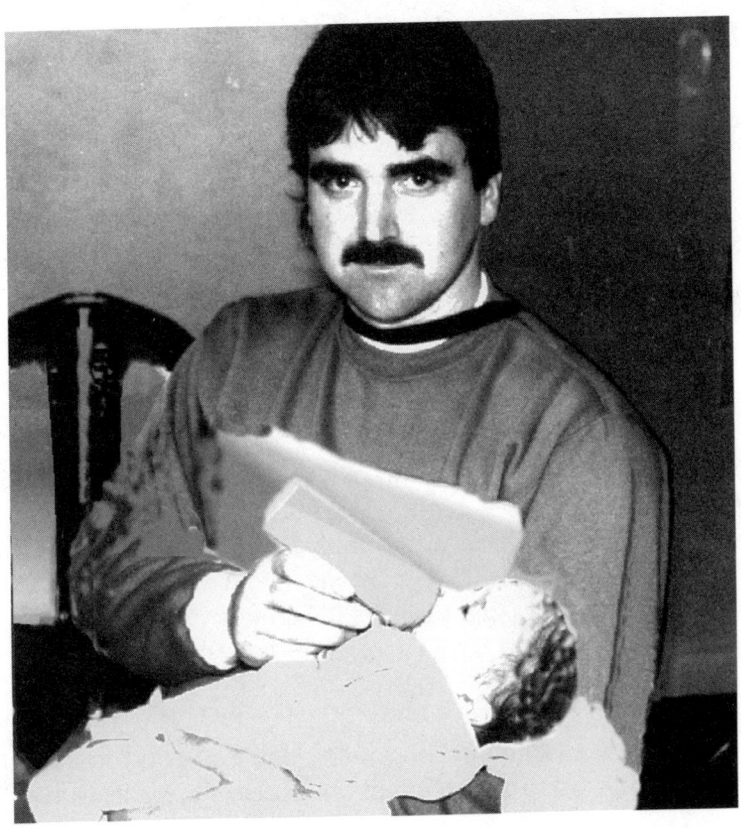

> **"We are bottle feeding so I get up at 1 A.M. and feed him so my wife can get a longer stretch of sleep.**
>
> **"We both had a difficult time adjusting to our baby's time clock. We are still trying to work out a routine where both of us could take turns and get more sleep."**

If you keep your baby in the same room with you, be prepared for the myriad of sounds you will hear. She will grunt, groan, sniffle, sputter, burp, and pass gas. Babies are little noise factories. You may want to put her in her own room from the beginning if she's disturbing what little sleep you're getting. Don't start any habits you won't want to continue for *years*, such as letting her sleep with you. It's hard to break those habits once they're established. Babies learn very early how to test the waters and limits. Their persistence is truly awesome when they don't want to give up something. Be forewarned.

> **"I'm having a difficult time adjusting to no sleep. I feel like I am walking around in a fog most of the time."**
>
> **"I didn't expect one little baby to be able to turn my life upside down."**
>
> **"We weren't prepared for all the different noises she made. At first we were afraid there was something wrong."**

BABY TALK

Your baby is ready from birth to start interacting with you. She isn't the little lump you think she is. She can focus on objects 8 to 10 inches away, and within a short period of time, she can recognize mom and dad from the other faces in her life. Babies prefer to look at faces rather than objects. Notice that she can mimic your expressions when you're smiling, frowning, and even sticking out your tongue. Babies love faces that are expressive and prefer voices with a high pitch. Communication from the first day is very important, so take advantage of every opportunity.

Few people can resist interacting with a baby. You'll find your normally deep voice rising to soprano just to get her attention. You can't help it. During her awake times, put her in her baby carrier or infant seat where she can see you as you putter around the house. Talk to her while you change and bathe her. She can actually discriminate between different types of sounds at a very early age. You can enhance her language development by using the correct word spoken in the correct way. In other words, don't use baby talk.

BURPS AND BATHS

Burping isn't a mysterious process. It can be easily done in several positions: upright over your shoulder, on his stomach over your lap, or with him leaning forward in a sitting position. Massage or stroke his back with the flat of your hand. Try burping in the middle of the feeding and again at the end. Sometimes it may be hard to hear the burp unless you use the over your shoulder position, where his mouth is near your ear. If you don't hear the burp, don't spend hours trying to make it happen. Put him on his stomach in his crib after you've finished the feeding.

Your baby doesn't get a regular bath until the umbilical cord heals and falls off. All you need to police up the area is a clean, warm washcloth to first wipe her eyes, then her head, behind her ears, face, neck, and chest. Regions below the belly button need more frequent cleaning to avoid irritation and diaper rash from contact with dirty/wet diapers.

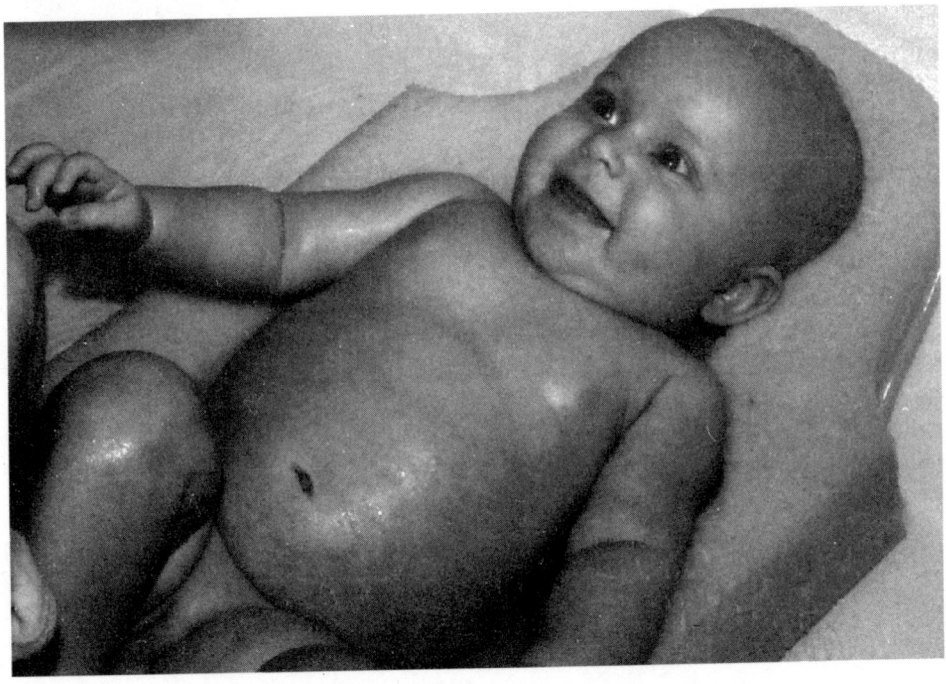

How Now

After the cord has fallen off, you can start regular baths in a baby tub, clean dishpan, or clean sink. Even small babies can be pretty squirmey and slippery. If you put a small towel or washcloth on the bottom, he won't slip and slide around. The tub needs only an inch or two of water, and the room should be warm. Use the same top-to-bottom washing sequence as before. About once a week you can wash his hair with a no-tears baby shampoo. If he has cradle cap (baby dandruff), use an adult dandruff shampoo and scrub with a soft brush. Don't worry about the "soft spot"; it isn't too soft to skip washing it. Lather his body from the neck down with a mild soap. Wash the penis or vaginal folds (labia) gently, just as you do the rest of the body. Don't use cotton-tipped sticks to wash anything! If you can't get to it with the corner of the washcloth, forget it. Rinse thoroughly from the neck down, and wrap him in a clean towel to dry.

Some babies love their baths from the start, but others take a little time to adjust. Some babies simply don't like having all their clothes and blankets off because it makes them nervous and so they put up a real fuss. You can help keep your baby calm by talking softly, keeping your hand securely under his neck, and avoiding hurried, jerky movements.

A bath every day for the first few months isn't a necessity. Two or three times a week is often enough for a full bath; after all, how dirty can a baby get in a day? Keep his hands clean, wipe off drools and dribbles, keep his bottom clean, and save your energy for other things.

SAFETY TIPS
Falls

Accidents from falls are easy to prevent. A little common sense goes a long way. Don't be tempted to put your baby on a countertop or changing table and leave her unattended and unsecured. Even small babies can manage to wiggle enough to fall. If you have to leave her even for a minute, put her on the floor.

Water Hazard

One-fourth of all childhood drownings occur at home in the bathtub. Never leave your baby alone while in the bathtub for any reason; even a few inches of water can be dangerous.

Siblings

Small children (1 to 4 years) are best not left alone with a new baby. Toddlers can't really distinguish the difference between the new baby and a doll. He can be hugged too hard or accidently dropped. Any time spent with the new baby should be supervised and enjoyable. The first few months are important bonding times for siblings too. They need to be able to interact with the baby at their own pace and when they show an interest. Forcing children to spend time with a new brother or sister delays bonding; it doesn't enhance it.

Pets

Pets shouldn't be allowed in the baby's room. Cats especially can be a problem because they love warm bodies, and what's more warm and snuggly than a baby? It's easy for a cat to jump into the baby's crib. There have been cases where a cat inadvertently smothered a baby. Well-mannered family dogs have bitten infants and small children without warning.

In general, the guidelines for protecting your baby from small children can be applied to pets. They can't be held responsible for what they don't understand. Don't tempt the fates.

URGENT URGES

As soon as things become more settled on the home front, your thoughts will return to the memories of past romantic encounters you shared with your wife. At this point you probably feel like sexual deprivation has become a way of life. Your hormones are heaving like the surf at high tide, and you're ready to hit the beach. You've experienced the famine, now you want to get on with the feast. When can you start rekindling the fire in her sexual furnace?

Doctors vary as to how long you should wait to resume intercourse. Few couples stick to the old 6 week limit. Some doctors advise waiting until the episiotomy heals, while others suggest a gentlemen waits until it's repaired. It doesn't matter because most couples succumb to temptation about the third week. One word of caution: if getting pregnant isn't high on your list, use some kind of birth control. Condoms plus foam is a good temporary method. Don't count on breast-feeding to keep her safe; it won't.

In spite of the go-ahead from her doctor, you may find her behaving like a reluctant virgin. It's normal for her to be a little gun-shy for as long as 3 months postpartum. Due to fatigue and decreased estrogen levels, she may not respond to sexual stimulation as quickly or as intensely as before. She can be more than a little fearful about intercourse hurting because of stitches and any other soreness she still feels. When you start getting reacquainted you'd be wise to treat her sexually as if she's starting all over. A good approach before plunging in is to use a lubricant such as K-Y jelly or Astroglide and insert one finger into her vagina and gently explore any potentially tender areas. If your exploration reveals any soreness, you can still rely on oral-genital methods until she feels better. If you can insert two fingers comfortably for her, intercourse should be relatively painless; it will help alleviate any apprehension she might feel. Let her assume the on-top position so she can control the amount of penetration. If she's apprehensive, keep the faith. Her libido, like the swallows to Capristrano, will indeed return again, and her response can be more intense than before due to the pregnancy effect that enhances sensitivity to the pelvic area; it provides the equivalent of a jump start for her engine.

Without some planning, resuming your love life can be fraught with hazards. Babies come with built-in radar that lets them know when you're otherwise engaged and choose that time to demand some attention. Make a date with each other for a time when you aren't tired or otherwise preoccupied. Get someone to take the baby for a few hours so you can be totally alone. You don't want any distractions at critical moments. It is extremely important to set aside this time for just the two of you. While things are getting back to normal, approach your love life with romance and a sense of fun and you can't go wrong. Be patient. Be positive.

A TIME FOR US

Trying to meet your new baby's needs and maintaining some balance in your relationship is a tough assignment, but not impossible. One of the biggest factors a baby alters in your relationship is spontaneity. You find you have to plan for everything, and you'll find yourself missing the more carefree times when you could just pick up and go. Now, even a trip to the grocery store is a big event. This is a major life change, but with care, consideration, thought, and especially planning you can make a smooth transition to familyhood without sacrificing your needs as individuals and as a couple. Here are a few plan-ahead tips that will help you in the first few weeks.

> "I didn't expect a baby to so totally take over our lives. We hardly have time to talk to one another except about her. Hopefully everything will return to normal after a few months."

Check out the better TV dinners and take out places BB (before baby). Stock up on critical items to eliminate trips to the store. Tell your friends you want gift certificates for free baby-sitting. Screen visitors for at least the first week because you'll both be tired enough without the added stress of entertaining people. Set times for visits with friends and family in advance when it's convenient for *you*. This isn't a time for houseguests. Pass on cousin Homer's request to hang out between jobs. If Grandma wants to come and help, make sure your wife really wants her to do that. Sometimes it's more stressful just having an extra person in the house, no matter who they are. People mean well, but they forget what it's like with a new baby at home. Hire a needy teenager to help around the house; they usually need the work and are used to minimum wages. Do whatever it takes to simplify your life in those first few weeks until you've settled into your new family routine.

> **"If I were to do it again, I would insist on no company for the first 2 weeks. It exhausted both of us.**

You, your wife, and baby have been through an exhausting, stressful, fun, exciting, life changing experience. You're beginning your new life as a family. Be patient and loving with each other, and above all, for the years to come, keep your sense of humor!

ΔΔΔ

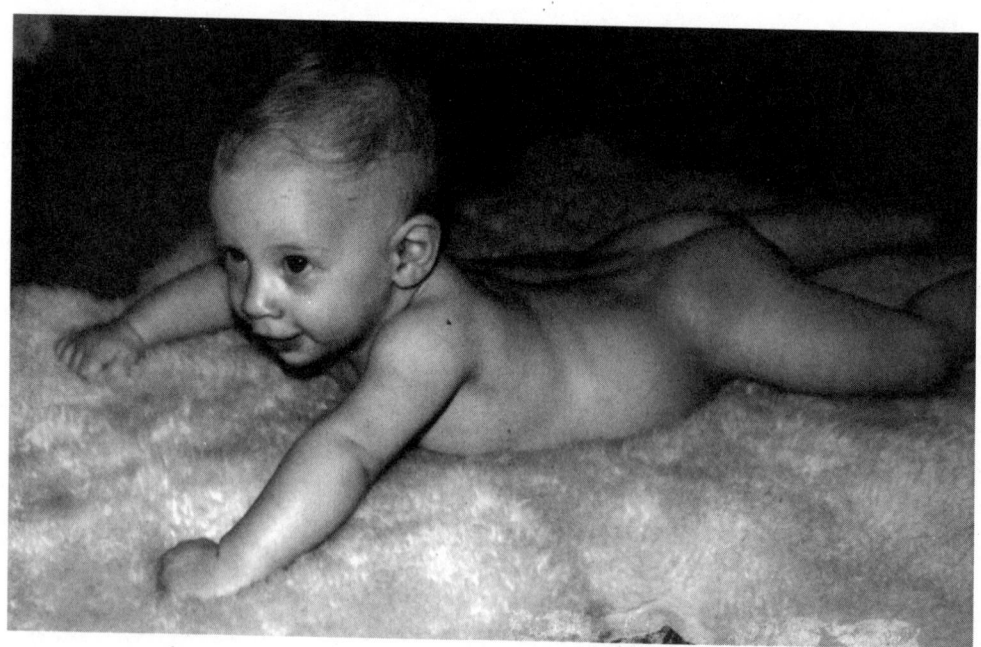

APPENDIX 1

RECOMMENDED RESOURCES

PREGNANCY AND BIRTH PREPARATION
Books

FROM HERE TO MATERNITY. Marshall, 1991. Comprehensive resource book for the pregnant couple. Informative, up-to-date, humorous guide through pregnancy from the beginning to the first six weeks at home with the baby. Conmar Publishing Inc.

CONFESSIONS OF AN EXPECTANT FATHER. Dan Greenburg. A touching and humorous account of one expectant father's experiences of pregnancy, birth and beyond.

A CHILD IS BORN. NILSSON, 1977. Actual photographs of the fetus from conception to birth.

MAKING LOVE DURING PREGNANCY. Bing and Coleman, 1982. Illustrated guide that discusses sex during pregnancy, myths, emotional aspects, and how to accomodate the changes that pregnancy brings.

THE MASSAGE BOOK. Downing, 1972. A beginner's guide to giving and receiving massage. A great way for you and your wife to connect emotionally and physically.

BIRTH—THROUGH CHILDREN'S EYES. Anderson and Simkin, 1977. Guide to preparing siblings for labor and birth. Well illustrated.

INFANT MASSAGE. Schneider, 1982. A well-done guide that includs basic techniques and application for problems such as colic.

PEACE OF MIND DURING PREGNANCY: AN A-Z GUIDE TO THE SUB-STANCES THAT COULD AFFECT YOUR UNBORN BABY. C. Kelly-Buchanon. An experienced teratogen counselor presents an overview of birth defects, and prenatal diagnosis techniques. She summarizes possible risk from individual substance exposures in pregnancy such as commonly prescribed drugs and specific teratogenic infections, chmical exposures, pesticides, and vaccinations. Environmental influences such as x-rays, microwaves, high altitude, pregnancy exercise and tanning booths.

HAVING A CESAREAN BABY. Hausknecht and Rattner-Heilman, 1983. Informative guide to cesaran birth.

PREVENTING PRETERM BIRTH: A PARENT'S GUIDE. Katz, Gill, & Turiel, 1988. The best book on preterm labor from prevention to delivery.

NEW HOPE FOR PROBLEM PREGNANCIES. Hales and Creasy, 1984. Discusses the carious high risk pregnancy conditions and their treatment.

FOOD VALUES OF COMMONLY USED PORTIONS. Pennington. 1989. A valuable resource for evaluating foods for calories, proteins, carbohydrates, and minerals such as calcium.

COMMUNICATION AND SELF-HELP

YOU JUST DON'T UNDERSTAND. Tannen. Helpful guide to improving your communication patterns with your mate.

THE INTIMATE ENEMY. Bach and Wyden. An insightful and entertaining book that teaches how to communicate more effectively and fight fairly with your mate.

IRON JOHN—THE STORY OF MEN. Bly, 1990. An historical look at male initiation from a mythological point of view. A great book to provide insights into male relationships and fathering.

HOMECOMING: Championing Your Inner Child. John Bradshaw, 1990. The first step to becoming a nurturing parent. You learn to identify, confront, and resolve any old issues you have from childhood. Highly recommended.

Video Tapes

ACOG Childbirth Preparation Program. A good supplement to childbirth classes or for those who need a brush-up course. Includes techniques for relaxation, massage, breathing, and visual imagery. The video version contains brief highlights from fourteen actual labors and births.

The ACOG Pregnancy Exercise Program. Nice gift for your wife. Provides safe exercises for the pregnant woman.

Kathy Smith Pregnancy Workout. Sybervision #6012. 90-minute video on how to relieve minor discomforts of pregnancy and get back into shape after the baby is born. Especially recommended. 1-800-777-5885

Baby Basics. Gives you a head start on caring for your baby. Video Health Communications. 1-800-526-4773 to order.

PARENTING

BETWEEN FATHER AND CHILD: How To Become The Kind of Father You Want To Be. Ronald Levant & John Kelly, 1989. The tools to communicating effectively with your child and how to balance discipline and nurturing needs. Excellent. Viking Penguin Press.

CARING FOR YOUR BABY AND YOUNG CHILD—BIRTH TO AGE 5. The American Academy of Pediatrics, 1991. Absolutely the best book on baby care and child development. It has everything you need to know. If you only buy 1 book, this should be it.

THE WORKING PARENTS SURVIVAL GUIDE. Sally Wendkos Olds, 1989. A comprehensive guide to the perils, pitfalls, and pearls for working parents written in a warm style. Prima Publishing.

THE VERY BEST CHILDCARE AND HOW TO FIND IT. Danalee Buhler, 1989. The ins and outs of day care, live-in help, basic health and safety from newborns to childrens 3 years of age. St. Martin's Press.

RAISING SELF-RELIANT CHILDREN IN A SELF-INDULGENT WORLD. H. Stephen Glenn & Jane Nelsen, 1989. The tools and building blocks to help your child develop into a capable and responsible person. St. Martin's Press.

PURCHASES

GUIDE TO BABY PRODUCTS by Consumer Reports Books, 1988. An invaluable aid to making the right decisions regarding baby equipment. The safety features and economics of all the various types of equipment available are covered.

APPENDIX 2

PRENATAL GENETIC SCREENING
HISTORY QUESTIONNAIRE*

NAME_____ DATE_____

QUESTIONS 1-5 pertain to both you and your wife.
Use space provided at the end of the questionnaire to explain yes answers.

Y N   1. Have either of you, or anyone in your families had any of
            the following disdorders?
Y N   a. Down's syndrome (mongolism)
Y N   b. Chromosomal abnormality
Y N   c. Neural tube defect (abnormality of spinal column such as
               spina bifida, open spine or anencephaly)
Y N   d. Hemophilia (blood clotting disorder)
Y N   e. Muscular dystrophy
Y N   f. Cystic fibrosis
Y N   g. Mental retardation
Y N   h. Any other birth defects or family disorders not listed above?
Y N   2. Have either of you had any children, dead or alive, from previous
            marriages or relationships with a birth defect not listed above?
Y N   3. As a couple, or with previous partners, have you had a stillborn
            child or three or more miscarriages in the first three months of
            pregnancy?
Y N   4. Have either of you had a chromosomal study?
        5. If either of you are of the following ancestry, have you been
            screened for any of these diseases?
Y N   a. Jewish_____Tay- Sachs
Y N   b. Black_____Sickle Cell
Y N   c. Mediterranean background
               Italian, Greek, etc. _____Thalassemia
Y N   d. Southeast Asian
               Chinese, Phillipine_____Thalassemia
Y N   6. When your baby is born, will your wife be 35 years or older?
Use space provided below to answer "YES" questions.

_____
_____
_____
_____

Adapted from the American College of Obstetricians and Gynecologists Technical bulletin
105-September 1987.

ABOUT THE AUTHOR

Connie Marshall is the mother of two and a clinical nurse specialist with a Master's degree in high-risk obstetrics. She has written numerous articles and books for both healthcare professionals and consumers. She is co-founder of a publishing company and consulting firm that provides and recommends educational materials to promote maternity wellness.

Additional Books by the Author:

From Here to Maternity

A comprehensive, up-to-date, 291-page guide for the pregnant couple. This book is written in a warm, witty style that is reassuring, and informs as it entertains. It guides you through the 9-month journey through pregnancy and stays with you for the first 6 weeks at home with the baby. A must for all pregnant couples. Recommended and used by healthcare professionals across the country.

De Aquí a La Maternidad

A user-friendly pregnancy guide especially for the Hispanic family. Written with warmth and sensitivity, it combines up-to-date information with cherished pregnancy and birth practices from the Hispanic culture.

For ordering information see coupon in back of this book or contact:

Conmar Publishing, Inc.
P.O. Box 641
Citrus Heights, CA 95611
1-800-428-8321

INDEX

A

ABO incompatibility
abdominal pain,
acetaminophen
    use in pregnancy, 31
accidents
    baby, 49
    mother, 96
acquired immunodeficiency syndrome (AIDS), 56
ADA diet, 82
adjustments
    prenatally, 3
    postpartum,145
aerobic exercise, 33
AFP (serum alpha fetoprotein), 104
alcohol
    use in pregnancy, 31
alpha fetoprotein (AFP), 104
amniocentesis, 102
    uses for, 103
amniotic fluid
    weight of, 18
analgesia
    for labor and delivery
        demerol, 125, 143
        morphine, 143
        stadol, 143
anesthesia
    epidural, 67, 125
    general, 137
    local, 133
    for circumcision, 43
antacids
    use in pregnancy, 331

anxiety
    effects of contractions, 125
Apgar score, 135
appointments, doctor, 57
aquafitness, 33
aspirin
    use in pregnancy, 31
axillary temperature (baby), 48

B

baby
    Apgar score, 135
    appearance of newborn, 133
    axillary temperature, 48
    baths and, 157
    belly button, 157
    bonding, 8, 21, 138
    bottle-feeding, 42
    breast-feeding, 39
    burping, 157
    car seats, 49
    changing table, 50
    clothing, 47
    circumcision
        procedure, 43
    comfort measures, 154
    cradle cap, 158
    crib, 49
    crying, 153
    dad's role, 151
    diapers, 47
    drowning, 158
    equipment, 45
    eye drops at birth, 136

F

G

H

I

nightmares, 26
nipple stimulation
    with breast-feeding, 41
    with intercourse, 13
nonstress test (NST), 100
nubain, 143
nutrition
    during pregnancy, 27

O

obstetrician, 97
oxytocin
    augmentation in labor, 111
    for induction of labor, 94
    release with nipple stimulation, 100
oxytocin challenge test (OCT), 100
orgasm, 13, 41, 161
overdue pregnancy, 94

P

pacifiers, 154
pain
    abdominal, 95
    headache, 19, 95
    heartburn, 25
    hemorrhoids, 25
    in labor, 122, 125
    round ligament, 24
    urinary infection, 89, 96
    varicose veins, 23
    with circumcision, 43
parenting, prepared, 73
    dysfunction, 77
    positive, 78
    trends, 73
parvovirus, 56
pediatrician, choosing, 44
penis, circumcision, 43

perinatal center, 97
perinatologist, 97
personnel, healthcare, 97
pets, and newborn, 160
placenta
    weight of, 18
positions
    for labor and birth, 129
    for sex, 14, 161
postdates pregnancy, 94
postpartum
    adjustments
        maternal, 145
        father, 140
        sexual, 160
        sleep deprivation, 145
    early days, 145
    blues, 147
    depression, 147
    siblings, 159
preeclampsia
    facts and myths, 85
    symptoms, 86
    treatment, 86
pregnancy
    after 35, 115
    postdates, 94
    products of, 18
prelabor, 121
prenatal workup, 54
prepared childbirth
    classes, 61
    evolution of, 59
    theory of, 61
preterm labor
    home monitoring of, 88
    symptoms, 89
    risk factors for, 88
problems in pregnancy, 81
products of pregnancy, 18

chorionic villus sampling, 103
contraction stress, 100
CMV (cytomegalovirus), 56
fetal acoustic stimulation (FAS),
101
    fetal, 99
    genetic, 102
    hepatitis, 57
    HIV (human immunodeficiency
virus), 56
    Kleihauer-Betke, 96
    magnetic resonance imaging
    (MRI), 106
    measles, 55
    nonstress, 99, 100
    oxytocin challenge, 100
    parvovirus, 56
    rubella (measles), 55
    serology, 55
    serum alpha fetoprotein (AFP),
    104
    toxoplasmosis, 57
    ultrasound, 104
    urinalysis, 55
    VDRL (serology), 55
temperature
    baby, 48
    maternal, 95
toxoplasmosis, 57
transition stage of labor, 130
travel, 36
twins, 90
tylenol
    use in pregnancy, 31

U

ultrasound
    safety of, 104
    uses for, 105

urinary tract infection, 89, 96
urine testing, 58
uterine
    cramping
        after amniocentesis,102
        after intercourse, 14

    incisions
        classical, 115
        episiotomy, 133
        low cervical, 115
uterus
    size, 58
    weight of, 18

V

vacuum extractor
    for delivery, 110
vaginal birth after cesarean (VBAC),
225
vaginal bleeding, 94
varicose veins, 23
vibrator
    use in pregnancy, 15
video display terminals (VDT), 36
vistaril, 143
vitamin supplements, 30
vomiting, persistent, 95

W

walking
    exercise during pregnancy, 33, 34
water pills, 22
weight gain, maternal, 29, 30, 58
weight, products of pregnancy, 18
weight training
    during pregnancy, 35
working
    during pregnancy, 36

Y

yoga
exercise during pregnancy, 35

Z

zoster immune globulin (ZIG), 55

OTHER SUCCESSFUL PARENTING BOOKS
FROM PRIMA PUBLISHING

From Here to Maternity
by Connie Marshall, R.N.

This exceptional book has become one of the most highly recommended by physicians and health organizations. The reason is simple: Without compromising on up-to-date medical information, it manages to inform pregnant couples with humor, warmth, and sensitivity. Connie Marshall covers all stages of pregnancy, delivery, and postpartum.
$9.95

The Very Best Child Care and How to Find It
by Danalee Buhler

This is the first book to focus on child care for infants and toddlers (from birth to three years old). Danalee is herself a mother and a child care professional. Included are topics ranging from different types of child care (the advantages and disadvantages) to basic health and safety issues—including checklists.
$8.95

Raising Self-Reliant Children in a Self-Indulgent World
by H. Stephen Glenn and Jane Nelsen, Ed.D.

As renowned educators whose seminars are attended by over 250,000 people annually, Stephen Glenn and Jane Nelsen offer a fresh approach to raising children. In this book you'll learn why so many children today feel irrelevant and alienated. Why, when you give them everything you never had, they appear ungrateful. But most of all, you will learn how to involve your children in activities and discussions that will help them feel capable and worthwhile.
$10.95

Bargains-by-Mail for Baby and You
by Dawn Hardy

Over 400 pages of mail-order companies with merchandise for children at budget-stretching savings offer the reader wonderful bargains. Educational products, toys and games, safety devices and handy gadgets, clothing, furniture, and resources for special needs, including products for the physically challenged, make this book a useful tool and reference for every family.
$14.95

FILL IN AND MAIL...TODAY

PRIMA PUBLISHING
P.O. Box 1260MAR
Rocklin, CA 95677

USE YOUR VISA/MC AND ORDER BY PHONE
(916) 786-0449
Mon.–Fri. 9-4 PST (12–7 EST)

I'd like to order copies of the following titles:

_____ copies of **The Expectant Father** at $10.95 each for a total of .... _____

_____ copies of **From Here to Maternity** at $9.95 each for a total of .... _____

_____ copies of **De Aquí a La Maternidad** (Spanish version of
From Here to Maternity) at $9.95 each for a total of.................... _____

_____ copies of **The Very Best Child Care** at $8.95 each for a total of......... _____

_____ copies of **Raising Self-Reliant Children** at $10.95 each for a total of..... _____

_____ copies of **Bargains-by-Mail** at $14.95 each for a total of................. _____

Subtotal.................................	_____
Postage & Handling.....................	**$4.00**
CA Sales Tax 7.25%.....................	_____
TOTAL (U.S. Funds only)...............	_____

☐ Check or Money Order enclosed for $_____, payable to Prima Publishing

Charge my ☐ Mastercard ☐ VISA

Account No. _____ Exp. Date _____

Signature _____

Your Name_____

Address _____

City/State/ Zip _____

Daytime Telephone _____

GUARANTEE
YOU MUST BE SATISFIED!
You get a 30-day, 100% money-back guarantee on all books.
Thank you for your order.

How did you hear about this book?

☐ Bookstore ☐ Other _____